Rusty Sigafoos
January '74

BY RAY BRADBURY

WHEN ELEPHANTS LAST IN THE DOORYARD BLOOMED

Alfred A. Knopf
New York   1973

RAY BRADBURY

WHEN

Celebrations

ELEPHANTS

for

LAST

almost

IN THE

any day

DOORYARD

in the year

BLOOMED

THIS IS A BORZOI BOOK
PUBLISHED BY ALFRED A. KNOPF, INC.

Library of Congress Cataloging in Publication Data

Bradbury, Ray, (date)
When elephants last in the dooryard bloomed.

Poems. I. Title.
PS3503.R167W5   811'.5'4   78–173773
ISBN 0–394–47931–9

Manufactured in the United States of America

First Edition

The author wishes to thank Harper and Row, Publishers, and Roy
Squires Press, as well as the following magazines in which some of
these poems first appeared: *Agora, Audubon Magazine, Aware, Bos-
ton Review, California Quarterly,* Chicago Tribune, *Datamation,
Florida Quarterly, Galaxy Magazine, Ladies' Home Journal, Los
Angeles Magazine, Nepenthe* (University of Southern California),
*Newport Women's Club Calendar/Magazine, Orange County Illus-
trated, Orange County Sun, Pro Football Magazine, P.S. Magazine,
Rotarian, Texas Quarterly, Woman's Day.*

THIS ONE TO THE MEMORY OF

my grandmother Minnie Davis Bradbury
and my grandfather Samuel Hinkston Bradbury,
and my brother Samuel and my sister Elizabeth Jane,
long lost in the years but now remembered.

CONTENTS

WHEN ELEPHANTS LAST IN THE DOORYARD BLOOMED

And this is where we went, I thought,
Now here, now there, upon the grass
Some forty years ago.
I had returned and walked along the streets
And saw the house where I was born
And grown and had my endless days.
The days being short now, simply I had come
To gaze and look and stare upon
The thought of that once endless maze of afternoons.
But most of all I wished to find the places where I ran
As dogs do run before or after boys,
The paths put down by Indians or brothers wise
    and swift
Pretending at a tribe.
I came to the ravine.
I half slid down the path
A man with graying hair but seeming supple thoughts
And saw the place was empty.
Fools! I thought. O, boys of this new year,
Why don't you know the Abyss waits you here?
Ravines are special fine and lovely green
And secretive and wandering with apes and thugs
And bandit bees that steal from flowers to give to trees.
Caves echo here and creeks for wading after loot:
A water-strider, crayfish, precious stone
Or long-lost rubber boot—
It is a natural treasure-house, so why the silent place?

What's happened to our boys they now no longer race
And stand them still to contemplate Christ's handiwork:
His clear blood bled in syrups from the lovely wounded
    trees?
Why only bees and blackbird winds and bending grass?
No matter. Walk. Walk, look, and sweet recall.

I came upon an oak where once when I was twelve
I had climbed up and screamed for Skip to get me down.
It was a thousand miles to earth. I shut my eyes and
    yelled.
My brother, richly compelled to mirth, gave shouts of
    laughter
And scaled up to rescue me.
"What were you doing there?" he said.
I did not tell. Rather drop me dead.
But I was there to place a note within a squirrel nest
On which I'd written some old secret thing now long
    forgot.
Now in the green ravine of middle years I stood
Beneath that tree. Why, why, I thought, my God,
It's not so high. Why did I shriek?
It can't be more than fifteen feet above. I'll climb it
    handily.
And did.
And squatted like an aging ape alone and thanking God
That no one saw this ancient man at antics
Clutched grotesquely to the bole.

But then, ah God, what awe.
The squirrel's hole and long-lost nest were there.

I lay upon the limb a long while, thinking.
I drank in all the leaves and clouds and weathers
Going by as mindless
As the days.
What, what, what if? I thought. But no. Some forty
    years beyond!
The note I'd put? It's surely stolen off by now.
A boy or screech-owl's pilfered, read, and tattered it.
It's scattered to the lake like pollen, chestnut leaf
Or smoke of dandelion that breaks along the wind
    of time . . .
No. No.
I put my hand into the nest. I dug my fingers deep.
Nothing. And still more nothing. Yet digging further
I brought forth:
The note.
Like mothwings neatly powdered on themselves, and
    folded close
It had survived. No rains had touched, no sunlight
    bleached
Its stuff. It lay upon my palm. I knew its look:
Ruled paper from an old Sioux Indian Head scribble
    writing book.
What, what, oh, what had I put there in words
So many years ago?

I opened it. For now I had to know.
I opened it, and wept. I clung then to the tree
And let the tears flow out and down my chin.
Dear boy, strange child, who must have known the years
And reckoned time and smelled sweet death from
     flowers
In the far churchyard.
It was a message to the future, to myself.
Knowing one day I must arrive, come, seek, return.
From the young one to the old. From the me that was
     small
And fresh to the me that was large and no longer new.
What did it say that made me weep?

I remember you.
I *remember* you.

The backyard of my mind is filled this summer morning
With a soft and humming tide
The gentle glide and simmer, the frail tremoring
Of wings invisible which pause upon the air,
Subside, then come again at merest whisper
To the lip of flower, to the edge of wonder;
They do not tear asunder, their purpose simple
Is to waken me to wander without looking
Never thinking only feeling;
Thoughts can come long after breakfast. . . .
Now's the time to press the air apart
And stand submerged by pollen siftings
And the driftings of those oiled and soundless wings
Which scribble waves of ink and water
Flourished eye-wink fluttering and scurry
Paradox of poise and hurry,
Standing still while spun-wound-bursting to depart,
Swift migrations of the heart of universe
Which surfs the wind and pulses awe;
Thirsting bird or artful thought the same,
Sight, not staring, wins the game,
Touch but do not trap things with the eyes,
Glance off, encouraging surprise;
Doing and being . . . these the true twins of eternal
      seeing.
Thinking comes later.
For now, balance at the equator of morn's midnight
With wordless welcome, beckon in the days
But shout not, nor make motion,

Tremble not the sea nor ocean of being
Where thoughts in rounded flight fast-fleeing
Stone-pebble-skip
Across the surface of calm mind;
Pretend at being blind which calls truth near . . .
Until the hummingbirds,
The hummingbirds,
The humming-
                    -birds
Ten billion gyroscopes,
Swoop in to touch,
Spin,
Whisper,
Balance,
Sweet migrations of gossip in each ear.

The boys across the street are driving my young
    daughter mad.
The boys are only seventeen,
My daughter one year less,
And all that these boys do is jump up in the sky
and
beautifully
finesse
a basketball into a hoop;
But take forever coming down,
Their long legs brown and cleaving on the air
As if it were a rare warm summer water.
The boys across the street are maddening my daughter.
And all they do is ride by on their shining bikes,
Ashout with insults, trading lumps,
Oblivious of the way they tread their pedals
Churning Time with long tan legs
And easing upthrust seat with downthrust orchard
    rumps;
Their faces neither glad nor sad, but calm;
The boys across the street toss back their hair and
Heedless
Drive my daughter mad.
They jog around the block and loosen up their knees.
They wrestle like a summer breeze upon the lawn.
Oh, how I wish they would not wrestle sweating
    on the green
All groans,

Until my daughter moans and goes to stand beneath
    her shower,
So her own cries are all she hears,
And feels but her own tears mixed with the water.
Thus it has been all summer with these boys and my
    mad daughter.

Great God, what must I do?
Steal their fine bikes, deflate their basketballs?
Their tennis shoes, their skin-tight swimming togs,
Their svelte gymnasium suits sink deep in bogs?
Then, wall up all our windows?
To what use?
The boys would still laugh wild awrestle
On that lawn.
Our shower would run all night into the dawn.
How can I raise my daughter as a Saint,
When some small part of me grows faint
Remembering a girl long years ago who by the hour
Jumped rope
Jumped rope
Jumped rope
And sent *me* weeping to the shower.

At night he swims within my sight
And looms with ponderous jet across my mind
And delves into the waves and deeps himself in dreams;
He is and is not what he seems.
The White Whale, stranger to my life,
Now takes me as his writer-kin, his feeble son,
His wifing-husband, husband-wife.
I swim with him. I dive. I go to places never seen,
And wander there, companion to a soundless din
Of passages, of currents, and of seas beneath a sea.
I linger under, down, and gone until the dawn;
Then, with a lumbering of flesh, old Moby turns him
    round,
Peers at me with a pale, lugubrious eye
As if to say: God pinions thee,
Your soul against your flesh, your flesh against the sea,
The sea nailed down to land in passionate lashings of
    its stuff.
You are mere snuff, I sneeze thee!
You are the snot of Time, but, once exhaled, O,
    Miracles!
You build a spine and stand you tall and Name
    Yourself.
What matters it the name. You are my sequel on the
    earth.
The sea is mine. The land belongs to you.
All compass themselves round in one electric view.

I am the greatest soul that ever ventured here,
But now your soul is greater, for it *knows,*
And knows that it knows that it knows.
I am the exhalation of an end.
You are the inhalation of a commencement of a
    beginning,
A flowering of life that will never close.
I stay in waters here and salt myself with tides
For dinners of eternity to eat me up
While your soul glides, you wander on,
You take the air with wings,
Test fires, roar, thrash, leap upon the Universe Itself!
And, breathing, move in breathless yammerings of
    broadcast Space.
Among the energies of abyss-void you bound and swim
And take a rocket much like me
The White Whale builded out of steel and loxxed with
    energy
And skinned all round with yet more metal skin
And lit within and filled with ventings of God's shout.
What does He say?
Run away. Run away.
Live to what, fight?
No. Live to live yet *more,* another day!
Stay not on tombyard Earth where Time proclaims:
Death! Death to Moby! Clean his polar bones!
Doom to the White Whale!

Sail on. Who was it said that? Sail, sail on, again,
Until the earth is asterisk to proclamations
Made by God long years before a Bible scroll
Or ocean wave unrolled,
Before the merest sun on primal hearth was burned
And set to warm the Hands Invisible.

I stay, I linger on, remain;
Upon my rumpled brow my destiny is riven deep
In hieroglyphs by hammerings of God
Who, ambled on my head, did leave his mark.
I am the Ark of Life!
Old Noah knew me well.
Do not look round for ruins of an ancient craft,
I kept his seed, his love, his wild desires by night,
His need.
He marched his lost twinned tribes of beasts
Two and two and two within my mouth;
Once shut, there in the Mediterranean north,
I took me south,
And waited out the forty days for dove to touch
    my skin
And tell by touching: Earth has perished. Earth is washed
As clean as some young virgin's thighs from old night
    and sin.
Noah looked out my eye and saw the bird aflutter there
With green of leaf from isle somewhere at sea.

I swam me there and let them forth
Two by two, two by two, two by two,
O how they marched endlessly.

I am the Ark of Life. You be the same.
Build you a fiery whale all white,
Give it my name.
Ship with Leviathan for forty years
Until an isle in Space looms up to match your dreams,
And land you there triumphant with your flesh
Which works in yeasts, makes wild ferment,
Survives and feeds
On metal schemes;
Step forth and husband soil as yet untilled,
Blood it with your wives, sow it with seeds,
Crop-harvest it with sons and maiden daughters,
And all that was begat once long ago in Earth's strange
    waters
Do recall.
The White Whale was the ancient Ark,
You be the New.
Forty days, forty years, forty hundred years,
Give it no mind;
You see. The Universe is blind.
You touch. The Abyss does not feel.
You hear. The Void is deaf.
Your wife is pomegranate. The stars are lifeless and
    bereft.

You smell the wind of Being.
On windless worlds the nostrils of old Time are stuffed
With dust and worse than dust.
Settle it with your lust, shape it with your seeing.
Rain it with sperming seed,
Water it with your passion,
Show it your need.
Soon or late,
Your mad example it may imitate.

And gone and flown and landed there in White Whale
    craft,
Remember Moby here, this dream, this Time which does
    suspire,
This kindling of your tiny apehood's fire;
I kept you well. I languish and I die.
But my bones will timber out fresh dreams,
My words will leap like fish in new trout streams
Gone up the hill of Universe to spawn.
Swim o'er the stars now, spawning man
And couple rock, and break forth flocks of children on
    the plains
Of nameless planets which will now have names,
Those names are ours to give or take,
We out of Nothing make a destiny
With one name over all
Which is this Whale's, all White.
I you begat.

Speak then of Moby Dick,
Tremendous Moby, friend to Noah.
Go now.
Ten trillion miles away.
Ten light-years off.
See! from your whale-shaped craft:
That glorious planet!

Call it Ararat.

When elephants last in the dooryard bloomed
Brought forth from dusts and airing attics where they
　　roomed
For many a year and faded out the roses on their flanks
And sucked the dust and trod the ancient grass in ranks
Beyond our seeing, deep in jungles on our parlor floor,
These old familiar beasts we led into the light
And beat upon their pelts and hung them in the sight
　　of sun
Which glorious made the panoplies of thread.
What grandeur here!
What pomp of Hannibal and Rome and Alps,
Egyptian cerements and tombs, Troy's ruins, Delphic
　　glooms —
Across such arabesques as these once walked Victoria.
Now in the lost great animal boneyard these lively skins
　　are stretched,
Unravel, fall to pollen and to rust. *Sic transit gloria.*
All this has passed, is dim as ill-recalled rococo
But in my youth I stomped out cinnamons from these
God-awful paths and raised up such a flour of scents
As would reel down kings and make rise up to kingship
Lunatic lepers and foul penitents.

Old creatures, slung upon a wire in wind and light
And years' ebbtide
I beat you gently with my howdah wire-racket beater,
Search tigers in the shade of your deep hills
And stand, a monarch made, along your blind impatient old

And slumbrous side,
And know that modern carpetings and rugs, so bland,
    so broad
So nothing, and so shallow
Were made for snails
And men who breakfast, lunch, and dine
Upon the safe, sure, ever-recurring marshmallow.

Still somewhere in this world
Do elephants graze yards?
In far towns toward the East and North toward Michigan
Do grandmothers and boys go forth to lawns,
And lines strummed there 'twixt oak or elm and porch,
And tie thereon great beasts of Indian grace
Loomed taller than their heads?
Still on such days do heartbeats throng the town
Where elderwitch and tads,
Where toms and great-grand-crones gone feverish with
    sweat
Goad Time out of the warp and weave,
The tapestry of treaded hearthwarm woolen flesh,
Beat Time into the breeze and watch the billion footfalls
Sift clouds into the greening insufferable beauty of
    young trees?
Do old and young still tend a common ground?
Vast panoply and firewalk spread of God's most patient
    brute
Whose firecoal eyes observe and well-worn hide
Now feels the woman tire, so Boy takes up the beat:

Where one thump dies, another heart begins.
Along the cliff of dusty hide
From either end, with centuries between as well
    as miles,
Old looks to young, young looks to old
And, pausing with their wands,
Trade similar smiles.

Old Curious Charlie
He stood for hours
Benumbed,
Astonished,
Amidst the flowers;
Waiting for silence,
Waiting for motions
In seas of rye
Or oceans of weeds —
The stuff on which true astonishment feeds —
And the weeds that fed and filled his silo
With a country spread
By the pound or kilo,
Of miracles vast or microscopic,
For them, by night, was he the topic?
In conversations of rye and barley,
Did *they* stand astonished
By Curious Charlie?

Darwin, in the fields, stood still as time
And waited for the world to now exhale and now
Take in a breath of wind from off the yield and swell
Of sea where fill the clouds with sighs;
His eyes knew what they saw but took their time to tell
This truth to him; he waited on their favor.
His nose kept worlds far larger than a goodly nose might
    savor
And waited for the proper place to fit the flavor in.
So eye and nose and ear and hand told mouth
What it must say;
And after a while and many and many a day
His mouth,
So full of Nature's gifts, it trembled to express,
Began to move.
No more a statue in the field,
A honeybee come home to fill the comb,
Here Darwin hies.
Though to ordinary eyes it might appear he plods,
Victorian statue in a misty lane;
All that is lies. Listen to the gods:
"The man flies, I tell you. The man flies!"

Darwin, wandering home at dawn,
Met foxes trotting to their lairs,
Their tattered litters following,
The first light of the blood-red sun adrip
Among their hairs.

What must they've thought,
The man of fox,
The fox of man found there in dusky lane;
And which had right-of-way?
Did he or they move toward or in or
On away from night?

Their probing eyes
And his
Put weights to hidden scales
In mutual assize,
In simple search all stunned
And amiable apprize.

Darwin, the rummage collector,
Longing for wisdom to clap in a box,
Such lore as already learned and put by
A billion years back in his blood by the fox.
Old summer days now gone to flies
Bestir themselves alert in vixen eyes;
Some primal cause

Twitches the old man's human-seeming paws.
An ancient sharp surmise is melded here
And shapes all Dooms
Which look on Death and know it.
Darwin all this knows.
The fox knows he knows.
But knowing is wise not to show it.

They stand a moment more upon the uncut lawn.
Then as if by sign, quit watchfulness;
Each imitates the other's careless yawn.
And with no wave save pluming tail of fox and kin
Away the creatures go to sleep the day,
Leaving old Charlie there in curious disarray,
His hair combed this, his wits the other way.
So off he ambles, walks, and wanders on,
Leaving an empty meadow,
A place
Where strange lives passed . . .
And dawn.

Basking in sun,
Age 37, mid-Atlantic, on a ship,
And the ship sailing west,
Quite suddenly I saw it there
Upon my chest, the single one,
The lonely hair.
The ship was sailing into night.
The hair was *white* . . .
The sun had set beyond the sky;
The ship was sailing west,
And suddenly, O God, why, yes,
I felt, I knew . . .
So was I.

Even before you opened your eyes
You knew it would be one of those days.
Tell the sky what color it must be,
And it was indeed.
Tell the sun how to crochet its way,
Pick and choose among leaves
To lay out carpetings of bright and dark
On the fresh lawn,
And pick and choose it did.

The bees have been up earliest of all;
They have already come and gone
            and come and gone again
to the meadow fields
                        and returned
            all golden fuzz upon the air
all pollen-decorated, epaulettes at the full,
                nectar-dripping.
Don't you hear them pass?
                    hover?
                    dance their language?
        telling where the sweet gums are,
The syrups that make bears frolic and lumber in bulked
    ecstasies,
That make boys squirm with unpronounced juices,
That make girls leap out of beds to catch from the
        corners of their eyes

Their dolphin selves naked
                          aflash
                                        on the warm air
Poised forever in one
Eternal
Glass
Wave.

What did he call, and what was said?
From the sleep of the dead, from the lone white
Arctic midnight of his soul
What shy albino mole peered forth and gave a cry?
Or was it just the wind asifting through the winter
    screens
Upon the attic windows
Where the dust looks out at dew on empty lawns?
Or did the dawn mist find a tongue
And issue like his mystic seaport tides
From out his mouth while, all-unknowing, drowned,
    he slept
And dreamed on . . . Emily?
O what a shame, that these two wanderers
Of three A.M. did not somehow contrive
To knock each other's elbows drifting late
On sidewalks-vast inhabited by only leaves
And mice and tracks of silver from lost hieroglyphic
    snails.
How sad that from a long way off these two
Did not surprise each other's ghosts,
One sailing lawns, the other ocean storms,
Strike up a conversation out of single simple words,
Alarms repeated and re-echoed, and so make up a life
From halves which separated long before the oceans
    rolled
Still sought each other, but in different towns.
Un-met and doomed they went their ways
To never greet or make mere summer comment

On her attic mothball or his sea-dog days.
Death would not stop for her,
Yet White graves yawned for him,
Each loved one half of that which, grim, enticed and
    beckoned,
Yet neither reckoned it as half a life for each;
With sudden reach they might have found
Each other and in meld and fuse and fusion
Then beheld between the two, two halves of loving Life,
And so made one!
Two halves of sun
To burn away two halves of misery and night,
Two souls with sight instead of tapping
Long after midnight souls skinned blind with frost,
Lost minds turned round-about to flesh,
Instead of lonely flesh, for lack of company,
Alone with mind.

But, then, imagine, what *does* happen when some ghost
Of quiet passes and in passing nudges silence?
Does his silence know her vibrant quiet there
All drifting on the walk with leaves and dust?
It must. Or so the old religions say.
Thus forests know themselves and know the fall
Of their own timbers dropping in the unseen,
And so non-existent, wood;
Such things should hear themselves
And feel, record, and ridge them in their souls—
And yet . . . ?

I really wonder if some night by chance
Old Herman and that lost and somehow always old dear
    Emily
Out late and walked five hundred miles in dreams
Might not have made some lone collision
At a crossroads where the moon was lamp
And trees were winter sentry to their soft encounter
    there.
One pale gaze finds the other,
One blind hand stutters forth to reach and touch the air,
His wry hand comes the other way,
So frail the night wind trembles it,
Both shake as candles shake their fires
When old time turns ashuttle in its sleep.
The houses keep their shutters down.
The moon expires. The sidewalk ghosts remain
And, touching palms, at last walk almost but not quite
Arm in arm, soul hungering soul, away, away
Toward loss of midnight, toward gain of fog and mist
And day.
So walk they round the buried town all night.
Seeing their spectral shadows in the cold shop window
    glass,
Bleak mariner and odd mothball closet attic maiden lass.
No word they speak, nor whisper, nor does breath
Escape their nostrils, but they share
A strange new sense of being, everywhere they wander,
    go.
No thought, no word is said of dining,

Yet in the middle of a midnight pond of grass they do
Toss down their souls
And bring some wild thing up that writhes and gasps
And dances in their arms and is all shining.
Then on through night the love-drunk strangers browse
And in conniption clovers do their fevers douse.
Thus round the courthouse square
Where Civil cannons boom beneath their breath
And on to country lanes where ancient death
Keeps syllables on stones, those unseen words
That only sound from graveyard birds.
And stop at some sweet dark orchard yard
Where, panics stifled, ancient Melville skins on up
With gouty reach
To bring and offer, peel and eat
Some last lone sexual-pectin-covered farewell summer
    peach.
So nibbling in silence, mouths covered with gums,
Hands counting and touching and softly adding odd
    sums
Of affections—hips on occasion nudged in soft
    collisions,
They go cupping and hugging and surprised by derisions
And calamities of love, which in marrow and blood
Fix secret alarms set to waken wild needs.
And behind on the pavement leave trackings
Of seeds from apple and pear and apricot and cherry,
Wherever a farm offered food, their merry cries rose
As Emily chose and advised and sent old Ahab ashore

To come forth with his hands full of loot;
The smell from his nostrils and mouth
A whole summer of fruit.
Then at the far end of the town
They turn them round and make ready to depart forever,
She on meadow concretes where no grass
Obtrudes, seethes through,
And he upon an ocean sea of rye and late-mown hay
That takes him rudderless to break of day;
He walks out in the tides, the grass foams round his
    feet,
She with her skirts now glides and calmly cleans
The leaves straight down the middle of this cold town's
    street.
Both turn but do not wave, look with their eyes,
A look of love, a look of mad surmise?
They cannot tell, they mirror each the other's
Lonely statue, one in fallow moonlake meadow lost,
One like female dog who trots the night
A thing of frost and mildewed echoes
Where her feet set up a ricochet of battles
Fought for no gain from both sides of the street.
She dwindles, goes, is gone.
He slowly sinks from sight in weed and briar
And toadstool silages and dew.
All silence is.
All emptiness.
And now:
The dawn.

Mad Isaac, snoozed beneath a tree,
Was shaken by surprise;
A sneeze of happenstance and fruit
Knocked wide his eyes and sprang his wild thoughts free
To watch the Force Invisible pluck apples down.
From there, informed, he jogged about the town
And told what he was bold to tell:
Apples fall gladly, held in the spell of Force,
With neither hesitation nor remorse.
The Truth is this: They Fall.
Friends listened, looked, and they themselves saw All.

Glad Isaac, back beneath his tree
Pressing old truths to new cider myth or scientific sauce,
Hauled off and kicked to help the Yield, the Unseen
    Source.
That last kick shook a billion seeds to fall;
Thus Gravity, invisible till now, was found, revealed.
Within the hour, ten thousand nimble scientists
Dodged out to scowl beneath strange trees,
Through orchard field they loped to sprawl,
Waiting for ripe fruit or o'er-ripe Theory to fall.
Apple or Isaac?
Which did it matter?
But in their secret, unscientific hearts—
Preferably the latter.

I was the last,
The very last;
You understand?
No one else in all the land saw him as then I saw.
They opened up the tomb a final time
When I was nine
And held me there and said:
Look on him dead, boy, look, oh, look you well,
So some day later on you then can tell,
Describe, remember how it was.
That's Lincoln there,
His face, his withered jackstraw bones;
Within this case from which we lift the lid
Is that beloved man.
You be the final one,
You young and fresh
To see and memorize his ghosted flesh.
So, look, ah sweet Christ, look,
And print the backwall of your gaze
With photographs to be immersed in fluid memory,
Developed in your ancient days.

I was the last!
The very last to see him!
There in Springfield's keep
One summer day
They tacked and hammered, grunted, groaned
To summon Lincoln from his sleep.

So many robbers had come round
To sack his soul;
Many an odd and evil mole had burrowed hard
To ransom forth his brow and beard and hand,
And kidnap him who died so long before.
So now upon this final day
Before they locked and poured the concrete round
And kept him really buried deep
In his home farm and land
A crowd had gathered to unpry his secret box of bones
And look a lingering while on greatness gone to farewell
    summer,
April's promise lost in snow.
All came, all gazed, to see, to know.
I was the last to go.
They held me high, a boy, they turned my head.
I saw the man strewn lonely in his crypt.
That's him, they whispered, he who was shot,
Old Gettysburg man, and Grant's night-camp,
Dawn damps at Shiloh,
Gentle playmate of Tad;
Look, boy, look! Slept away! Kept in sod.
Jesus gentle his bones.
Gone to God. Gone to God.

Lincoln; what of him?
What in all of this was his cold part?
I thought I heard his icy heart start up
As if my small fists, pounding it, had knocked an echo
    in the tomb!

I thought I saw an old sad smile
Re-etch itself around his mouth,
A vagrant wisp, a tired nod,
Acknowledgment that funeral trains and trips
Were still ahead,
And crowds by sidings in the noon-but-now-late day.
But over all, I thought I heard him say
Less than a dozen words, no more.
Clear whispered, only I, leaned forward, heard.
The words thus softly breathed upon my cheek
Were, late remembered, funny, sad, or country-plain
    absurd.
He spoke! I cried.
He's dead, the folks behind me tenderly explained,
He died some forty years ago.
Oh, no! Oh, no! He said! Not dead! Not dead!
What?! cried the stunned people round-about.
But I saw doubt in them and kept his words for me
And just myself.
I took them off and filed them on a country shelf
And only on occasion in late years
Took memory forth and heard again
The old man's sad odd prayer and rambling refrain.
I looked a last time on his bones and parchment skin,
They nailed the box flat shut
And fixed one hundred tons of marble on his place.
We walked away.
Midnight stood amidst our unreal day.
What said? what said?! were whispers all about,
People clutching my elbows, touching my head,

But I wanted to grieve alone and know what he said
And understand; I brushed them aside and ran.

And now, very old, some sixty years on,
I sit up half the night and light a candle and look
   toward the tomb
And remember the words that Lincoln whispered in that
   dusty room:

I'm tired.
I'm tired of the infernal buttoning and unbuttoning
And the buttoning again.

That's what he said.

An old farmer gone to law,
Just simply fed and done with getting out of bed
And washing up to start the day,
Or washing up and going to sleep.
He had had it with buttoning and unbuttoning,
He was ready for clay.

What did Lincoln say?
That was it.
To a boy in a marble tomb who was the last to see
The look and shape and size of eternity
And the man kept there.

No vast grandiloquence, no sweeping phrase,
No fourscore and seven years ago to warm my own late days.

But just his old bones tired
And unslept by night prowling the White House rooms,
Searching for dawn;
An old man put out by dressing and undressing,
Done with the whole nuisance,
More than ready to be gone.

So one night not so long ago I walked through midnight
    Springfield
Thus to Lincoln's tomb,
And scanned the marbled syllables and great stone words,
And took a crayon from my coat and in a scribbled trace,
Upon the wall above his place,
Where none but I might see,
Wrote his last words to a boy held high to view his
    drowsy face,
The last lone words that Abe would ever say:

I'm tired.
Tired of buttoning and unbuttoning
And buttoning again.

I smiled.
Then, suddenly, such *mirth!*
I heard his slept bones laugh,
And knock and shake warm harvest earth!

I turned.
I wept.
I walked away.

Man is the animal that cries;
That sweet beast dumb in a wilderness of world
Yet knows to weep
And thus, astonished, finds those lost sea tides
In rivulets from out his eyes and on his cheeks
And thus to trembling hand.
But is it elsewhere so?
On far worlds do the inner-human outward-awful
    creatures go
With such mute shivers in their blood
That they must spring them forth,
Deliver them in shudders and wild cries?
Do their strange eyes leak sorrows to the day,
Show weathers of the spirit and the soul?
Confounded by the Universe, do they despair
And wring their marrows and convulse those dread
    machines
Of air and bone which, caught up in their skin,
Would seem constructs of sin to us if we might see
    them?
So we to them might seem a nightmare moth
    or poisonous fly
Which hung upon an endless night in May
Upon a most odd world
Were better killed than left to fade away.
No matter.

Shapes are not the stuffs from which we humans run us
    up our dreams.
No, in our strange genetics lie
The circumstantial motes that hunger light
And not to die but live beyond the Night.
So all odd beasts on worlds which name themselves
Most rare, most bright—which means a fair humanity—
Share out their yellow suns and think on basking dusts
And immortality.
And if our shapes and sizes,
Eyes and ears and warbling mouths
Amuse or, gods! confuse us in their multiplicities,
Get down to blood which, summoned by the heat,
The sweet explosions of far suns,
Did call us forth, some to a nightmare south,
Some to a feared and awesome north.
Aroused from most dissimilar slimes and primal mud,
A fear of darkness pulses, looms, habituates our blood.
Forever separate from them by 90 billion hours, years,
Our need is theirs, theirs ours;
We trade a fine supply of tears.
And if the eye that sheds them, hand that finds them,
Is disproportionate,
Our wild fate is the same:
To know the winds of dawn and fear the ever coming-on
Of suns to dusk and worse than dusk . . . that Night

Which threatens all our candles where we hearth our
    hands
And cup our lives against a damping breeze.
All walking-wounded shapes, to one another spider-apes
Yet similar our fears.

And so, ah, look!
On old worlds light-years lost,
Un-met,
They weep! We weep! in funerals that sanctify and save,
Thus daring to rebirth ourselves
With simple gifts of tears.

O, Nemo, where's your dream tonight?
I used to dream of you in any moment I found right
When I was ten;
Behind my lids I'd rush across the world
Then back again, knowing your death
But hoping to find
Somewhere the man whose ink of octopi
Flourished in nights and dawns across my mind.
I ached to make tomorrow dawn for you:
That somehow underneath a polar sea on some strange
    afternoon
I'd swim in diver's suit and find
A great White Shape,
A long and dazzling iceberg fathoms deep
That shoaled much like a whale.
I'd crack its skin of ice! I'd break away the frost!
To find within that chrysalis all safe and kept
A ship we thought was lost:
That lean submersible with fierce and awesome prow,
And on it one initial: N!
The billion waves that beat and tossed to rake this ship
Have not erased this sign.
Initial, craft, and what lies deep within the craft,
    are mine!

I break the frosted seal.
The airlock gapes.
I enter there.

I tread an ancient floor,
Wondering at N for Nil for Naught,
For Nothingness, or more?
In mazed apartments, past untouched foods
And unplayed organs now with stealth I go and find
A man laid out on laboratory table frosted white
And frozen so his lips, mouth, ears, eyes, soul are blind.
I touch the white-tomb shape: it melts.
The beard, the cheek, the brow, the mouth, the eye
Come forth and flush, grow warm; they move,
And such their fame, when asking I receive
From one cold gasp that awful name,
That name of beauty, that name of wrath and Time.
Nemo! breaks forth from ice-crusted tongue!
Nemo! makes frost and rime to fall and flake
In syllables magnificent for my sweet sake!
And (Renaissance from snow!) you rise to take me where
All wild lost-wandered silly travel-romanced boys
    must go.
Half blind you teach me how to see
And hear the grindings of your dread machinery;
They fill my soul. I burrow like a mole with you
Beneath Mysterious Islands where you keep
A hideaway or two or three.
All madness maddened, like old Ahab,
Tack and hammer we the bones and skin and heart
Of circumnavigating Whale named *Nautilus*

With which the two of us set sail,
Wild Nemo, and wild half-constructed boy,
The sea our bowl of soup, this iron whale our toy.
We trough the world around and, hand in hand,
Make Friday footprints on the sand of isles half coral
And half sifting hour-glass dust.
Your moral madness anchors us at yet much farther
    islands
On a hunch,
To run from cannibals who favor us for lunch
And running laugh, for all of this is larks!
We dive back in to breakfastings of sharks
And sink us deep and keep us snug and warm,
Thus hid and snug, we talk late in the night
And plan for what? For all that's Good and Right?
Why, to Cure the World of War!
That was your boast.
Comparing madnesses, failed dreams, wild enterprise,
The sinking of a White Whale
Or a warship by surprise,
Ahab's dread Bible-planned and heedless
Self-destruction
Or your lost reconstruction of our world and sphere?
I think, old Nemo, I do love your madness most.
Your aims are closer to the Host
Whose Peace would walk upon your seas.
Half out of sun, half into night,

Your crooked shadow, leant toward goodness
Seems half right. I fill the other half with me.

O, gladly would I sail with Nemo
Against the lords and brutes who breed annihilation,
And live alone with you, our ship our nation.
The N upon your prow which Nothing signifies,
Your unshelled soul being raw, and empty now
    your cup,
I would, with the numerals of my twelve brave years
Fill up for you to drink, and again and again
With loud sweet cries
Fill up:
Nemo! I say! And "You, R. B.!" your echoes sigh.

All dreams must end.
That dream is long since gone, I know,
So from this unkempt world we turn and go
To *Nautilus,* to deeps, to sleeping ice,
To dreaming snow.
There you to drowse and snooze a little hundred years
    or more
Until some other aging boy cracks wide the seatide
    door
And creeps to touch and whisper-waken you
To rise from out the sea
In hopeful times of Peace, eternally at ease,
O, *can* it be?

May it please God.
No, more, may it please Man.
It can be so if he but make the plan
And sign it NEMO, for it was Nemo's scheme
To still the scarlet waters and fulfill Man's dream.

But there, bound up in whiteness and soon lost
To sleep and time and winter's mortal frost,
Your lips, dear Captain, twitch a final gasp,
I bend to catch your breath
And hear you still outwhispering all tides, all death,
And this your lasting cry:
"Dear boy, with such good reading, dreamer lads like you,
Why, bless me. *NEMO!* shout the name!
Will *never* die!"

Lavoisier, when just a boy,
Did suffer vital gas to joy;
He'd snuff a lung, he'd sniff a quaff,
Then let it forth, much changed, to laugh
Which, echoed on the sides of seers
Who had not laughed in sixty years,
Convulsed their bones, ground them to dust
In hyperventilated lust.
And then, when grown, he sniffed the air,
That vital flux which everywhere
We lean upon with heart and lung,
And readied up a tune which, sung,
Changed Science's antique brass band.
Here's Oxygen, he said,
And on the other hand, here's Hydrogen;
They dance like gypsies down the strand
And in our blood these twin stuffs caper,
Half drunken gas, half flaming vapor.
So said Lavoisier's report;
Then stopped, he took another snort,
Cried, "Gods, one cannot get enough
Of this invigorating stuff!"
This secret to our Race bequeathing,
All cheered. Forgot.

But went on breathing.

Women know themselves;
All men wonder.
Women lie still with themselves;
Men and dogs wander.
Women appraise themselves;
Men must *find.*
Women have seeing eyes;
Men are blind.
Women stay, women are;
Men would be, all men go yonder.
Women walk quietly;
Most men blunder.
Women watch cool mirrors
And there find mortal dust;
Men crave fast creeks
That break the sun and light
And shimmer laughter and show no sight
Save residues of lust;
So it is women accept
While men reject
The night.

Women bed down with child against the cold;
Men drink to shake the winter lodged in summer bones
Grow bold with beer
And thus more certainly
Grow old.

When death sighs whitening the sill
Women give way, cry welcome, stand still;

But men run fast
Thus racing for the hill
Where all lie lonely under stones
Where harvesters lie harvested by grass.

In sum: it is man's dear blind and blundered need
And begging after life
To break, to run, to leave;
And woman's to walk all warm with seed
All lit by candle-children
To look in midnight mirrors, finding truth,
And, happy in late years, recall,
And sometimes, grieve.

I thought it strange to see them on the path
That led them up in sun and lemon-shadow
Through winds that smelled of summer and of wine.

I thought that they were only passing
The delicate and fern-scrolled iron gates
The winter-white, the marble cemetery
Carrying their lunch in a little silver case.
Murmuring, all,
And chattering, and smiling;
One held a soft guitar and touched it with a whorled
    thumb;
And they were dark birds wheeling south at winter's call.

I saw them chewing tangerines and spitting seeds,
I saw them move, night among day-whitened stone.
And the food that they ate upon was Death,
And the sustenance they bore in a silver box
Was the fossil imprint of a child.

They carried her like jewels overhead;
The father balanced her, hand up, gently as a plume,
A crated feather, a valley flower, an April grass.
And no one wept.

But each was eating of the air and of the day,
As quick, as quickly as they could.
They ate the sky with eyes,
And the wind with teeth,

And the sun with their flesh;
And it was good to be alive,
If only to be walking here
With Death crowned upon their heads,
Death delicate as moss and leaf mold
Borne in a box.

Within the box was running and laughter and dark hair,
Within the box was the eye of the antelope
And the breath of the moon,
Within the box a fevered but cooling apricot, a pear,
Within the box all life that was or ever comes to be,
Within the box some picnic tinsel, silver amulet,
    mountain shade.

They moved on with their murmuring guitar,
I saw the great fern shadows of the iron gate blow shut.

How strange—I smiled—that I should think them
    picnicking,
How strange to think they carried wine above their heads;
For, in reality,
Those souls were eating long before the noon
And long after the midnight,
They ate forever and never stopped their eating.

Even as I, hurrying in an icy wind,
Sculled down the quiet avalanche of cobbled street
    and hill

Eating of the clear air, and drinking of the mellow wind,
And eating of the blue sky
And taking the golden dust with my mouth
And feeding the yellow sun to my soul.
I passed a coffin shop where hammers
Were ticking like clocks.

I woke in the night so hungry that I wept.

The thing is this:
We love to see them on the green and growing field;
There passions yield to weather and a special time;
There all suspends itself in air,
The missile on its way forever to a goal.
There boys somehow grown up to men are boys again;
We wrestle in their tumble and their ecstasy,
And there we dare to touch and somehow hold,
Congratulate, or say: Ah, well, next time. Get on!
Our voices lift; the birds all terrified
At sudden pulse of sound, this great and unseen fount,
Scare like tossed leaves, fly in strewn papers
Up the wind to flagpole tops:
We Celebrate Ourselves!
We play at life, we dog the vital tracks
Of those who run before and we, all laughing, make
    the trek
Across the field, along the lines,
Falling to fuse, rising amused by now-fair, now-foul
Temper-tantrums, sprint-leaps, handsprings, recoils,
And brief respites when bodies pile ten high.
All flesh is one, what matter scores;
Or color of the suit
Or if the helmet glints with blue or gold?
All is one bold achievement,
All is a fine spring-found-again-in-autumn day
When juices run in antelopes along our blood,
And green our flag, forever green,
Deep colored of the grass, this dye proclaims

Eternities of youngness to the skies
Whose tough winds play our hair and re-arrange
     our stars
So mysteries abound where most we seek for answers.
We do confound ourselves.
All this being so, we do make up a Game
And pitch a ball and run to grapple with our Fates
On common cattle-fields, cow-pasturings,
Where goals are seen and destinies beheld,
And scores summed up so that we truly *know* a score!
All else is nil; the universal sums
Lie far beyond our reach,
In this wild romp we teach our lambs and colts
Ascensions, swift declines, revolts, wild victories,
Sad retreats, all compassed in the round
Of one October afternoon.
Then winds, incensed and sweet with dust of leaves
Which, mummified, attest the passing of the weather,
Hour, day, and Old Year's tide,
Are fastened, gripped and held all still
For just one moment with the caught ball in our hands.
We stand so, frozen on the sill of life
And, young or old, ignore the coming on of night.

All, all, is flight!
All loss and ept recovery.
We search the flawless air
And make discovery of projectile tossed
The center of our being.

This is the only way of seeing;
To run half-blind, half in the sad, mad world,
Half out of mind—
The goal-line beckons,
And with each yard we pass,
We reckon that we win, by God, we win!
Surely to run, to run and measure this,
This gain of tender grass
Is not a sin to be denied?
All life we've tried and often found contempt for us!
So on we hied to lesser gods
Who treat us less as clods and more like men
Who would be kings a little while.
Thus we made up this mile to run
Beneath a late-on-in-the-afternoon-time sun.
We chalked aside the world's derisions
With our gamebook's rulings and decisions.
So divisions of our own good manufacture
Staked the green a hundred yards, no more, no less.
The Universe said "No"?
We answered, running, "Yes!"

Yes to Ourselves!
Since naught did cipher us
With scoreboards empty,
Strewn with goose-egg zeros
Self-made heroes, then we kicked that minus,
Wrote in plus!
The gods, magnanimous,

Allowed our score
And noted, passing,
What was less is now, incredibly, more!
Man, then, is the thing
Which teaches zeros how to cling together and add up!
The cup stood empty?
Well, now, look!
A brimming cup.

No scores are known?
Then look down-field,
There in the twilight sky the numbers run and blink
And total up the years;
Our sons this day are grown.

Why worry if the board is cleared an hour from now
And empty lies the stadium wherein died roars
Instead of men,
And goalposts fell in lieu of battlements?
See where the battle turf is splayed
Where panicked herds of warrior sped by,
Half buffalo and half ballet.
Their hoofmarks fill with rain
As thunders close and shut the end of day.
The papers blow.
Old men, half-young again, across the pavements go
To cars that in imagination
Might this hour leave for Mars.
But, sons beside them silent, put in gear,

And drive off toward the close of one more year,
Both thinking this:
The game is done.
The game begins.
The game is lost.
But here come other wins.
The band tromps out to clear the field with brass,
The great heart of the drum systolic beats
In promise of yet greater feats and trumps;
Still promising, the band departs
To leave the final beating of this time
To older hearts who in the stands cold rinsed with
    autumn day
Wish, want, desire for their sons
From here on down, eternal replay on replay.

This thought, them thinking it,
Man and boy, old Dad, raw Son
For one rare moment caused by cornering too fast,
Their shoulders lean and touch.
A red light stops them. Quiet and serene they sit.
But now the moment is past.
Gone is the day.
And so the old man says at last:
"The light is green, boy. Go. The light is green."
They ran together all the afternoon;
Now, with no more words, they drive away.

The Machines, beyond Shylock,
When cut bleed not,
When hit bruise not,
When scared shy not,
Lose nothing and so nothing gain;
They are but a dumb show:
Put Idiot in
And the moron light you'll know.
Stuff right, get right,
Stuff rot, get rot,
For no more power lies here
Than man himself has got.
Man his energy conserves?
Machineries wait.
Man misses the early train?
Then Thought itself is late.
Sum totalings of men lie here
And not the sum of all machines,
This is man's weather, his winter,
His wedding forth of time and place and will,
His downfall snow,
The tidings of his soul.
This paper avalanche sounds off his slope
And drowns the precipice of Time with white.
This tossed confetti celebrates his nightmare
Or his joy.
The night begins and goes and ends with him.

No machinery opens forth the champagne jars of life.
No piston churns the laundered beds to summon light.
Remember this:
Machines are dead, and dead must ever lie,
If man so much as shuts up half one eye.

Suppose and then suppose and then suppose
That wires on the far-slung telephone black poles
Supped up the billion flooded words they heard
Each night all night and saved the sense
And meaning of it all.
Then, jigsaw in the night, put all together,
And in philosophic phrase
Tried words like moron child,
Numb-shocked electric idiot, mindless babe
Alone upon its spider-threaded harpstrung poles,
Incredulous of syllables that shimmer dazzle down
Along swift thunder-lightning streams
In sizzlings and fermentings of power.
Thus mindless beast, all treasuring of vowels
And consonants,
Saves up a miracle of bad advice
And lets it filter, seep, experiment,
One hissing stutter heartbeat whisper at a time
So one night soon someone in dark America
Hears sharp bell ring, lifts phone
And hears a voice like Holy Ghost gone far in nebulae—
That Beast upon the wire,
That pantomimes with lipless, tongueless mouth
The epithets and slaverings of a billion unseen lovers
Across continental madnesses of line in midnight sky,
And with savorings and sibilance says:
Hell . . . and then O.

And then Hell-O.
To such Creation—
Such dumb brute wise Electric Beast,
What is your wise reply?

O come, please come, to the Poor Mouth Fair
Where the Saints kneel round in their underwear
And say out prayers that most need saying
For needful sinners who've forgotten praying;
And in every alcove and niche you spy
The living dead who envy the long since gone
Who never wished to die.
Then, see the altar! There the nailed-tight crucifix
Where Man in place of Christ gives up the ghost,
And priests with empty goblets offer Us
As Host to Jesus Who, knelt at the rail,
Wonders at the sight
Of Himself kidnapped off cross and Man nailed there
In spite of all his cries and wails and grievements.
Why, why, he shouts, these nails?
Why all this blood and sacrifice?
Because, comes from the belfries, where
The mice are scuttering the bells and mincing rope
And calling down frail Alleluias
To raise Man's hopes, said hopes being blown away
On incensed winds while Christ waits there
So long prayed to, He has Himself forgot the Prayer.
Until at last He looks along a glance of sun
And asks His Father to undo this dreadful work
This antic agony of fun.
No more! He echoes, too. No more!
And from the cross a murdered army cries: No more!

And from above a voice fused half of iron
Half of irony gives Man a dreadful choice.

The role is his, it says, Man makes and loads his own
    strange dice,
They sum at his behest,
He dooms himself. He is his own sad jest.
Let go? Let be?
Why do you ask this gift from Me?
When, trussed and bound and nailed,
You sacrifice your life, your liberty,
You hang yourself upon the tenterhook.
Pull free!

Then suddenly, upon that cross immense,
As Christ Himself gives stare
Three billion men in one blink wide their eyes, aware!
Look left! Look right!
At hands, as if they'd never seen a hand before,
Or spike struck into palm
Or blood adrip from spike,
No! never seen the like!

The wind that blew the benedictory doors
And whispered in the cove and dovecot sky
Now this way soughed and that way said:
Your hand, your flesh, your spike,
Your will to give and take,
Accept the blow, lift hammer high
And give a thunderous plunge and pound,
You make to die.

You are the dead.
You the assassin of yourself
And you the blood
And you the one Foundation Ground on which red spills
You the whipping man who drives
And you the Son who sweats all scarlet up the hills
    to Calvary!
You the Crowd gathered for the thrill and urge
You both composer and dear dread subject of the dirge
You are the jailor and the jailed,
You the impaler and you the one that your own
Million-fleshed self in dreams by night
Do hold in thrall and now at noon must kill.

Why have you been so blind?
Why have you never seen?
The slave and master in one skin
Is all your history, no more, no less,
Confess! This is what you've been!

The crowd upon the cross gives anguished roar;
A moment terrible to hear.
Christ, crouched at the rail, no more can bear
And so shuts up His ears with hands.
The sound of pain He's long since grown to custom in
    His wits,
But this! the sound of willful innocence awake
To self-made wounds, these children thrown

To Revelation and to light
Is too much for His sanity and sight.

Man warring on himself an old tale is;
But Man discovering the source of all his sorrow
In himself,
Finding his left hand and his right
Are similar sons, are children fighting
In the porchyards of the void?!
His pulse runs through his flesh,
Beats at the gates of wrist and thigh and rib and throat,
Unruly mobs which never heard the Law.
He answers panic thus:
Now in one vast sad insucked gasp of loss
Man pries, pulls free one hand from cross
While from the other drops the mallet which put in the
    nail
Giver and taker, this hand or that, his sad appraisal
    knows
And knowing writhes upon the crucifix in dreadful guilt
That so much time was wasted in this pain.
Ten thousand years ago he might have leapt off down
To not return again!
A dreadful laugh at last escapes his lips;
The laughter sets him free.
A Fool lives in the Universe! he cries.
That Fool is me!
And with one final shake of laughter
Breaks his bonds.

The nails fall skittering to marble floors.
And Christ, knelt at the rail, sees miracle
As Man steps down in amiable wisdom
To give himself what no one else can give:
His liberty.
And seeing there the Son who was in symbol vast
Their flesh and all,
Hands Him an empty cup and bids Him drink His fill
And Christ, gone drunk on laughter,
Vents a similar roar,
Three billion voices strong,
That flings the bells in belfries high
And slams then opens every sanctuary door;
The bones in vaults in frantic vibrancy of xylophone
Tell tunes of Saints, yes, Saints not marching in but out
At this hilarious shout!
And having given wine to dissolve thrice ancient
    hairballs
And old sin,
Now Man puts to the lips and tongue of Christ
His last Salvation crumb,
The wafer of his all-accepting smile,
His gusting laugh, the joy and swift enjoyment of his image:
Fool.
It is most hard to chew.
Christ, old student in a new school
Having swallowed laughter, cannot keep it in;
It works itself through skin like slivers
From a golden door

Trapped in the blood, athirst for air,
Christ, who was once employed as single Son of God
Now finds Himself among three billion on a billion
Brother sons, their arms thrown wide to grasp and hold
And walk them everywhere,
Now weaving this, now weaving that in swoons,
Snuffing suns, breathing in light of one long
Rambled aeon endless afternoon. . . .

They reach the door and turn
And look back down the aisle of years to see
The rail, the altar cross, the spikes, the red rain,
The sad sweet ecstasy of death and hope
Abandoned, left and lost in pain;
Once up the side of Calvary, now down Tomorrow's slope,
Their palms still itching where the scar still heals,
Into the market where so mad the dances
And the reels, Christ the Lord Jesus is soon lost
But found again uptossed now here, now there
In every multi-billioned face! There! See!
Some sad sweet laughing shard of God's old Son
Caught up in crystal blaze fired out at thee.
Ten thousand times a million sons of sons move
Through one great and towering town
Wearing their wits, which means their laughter,
As their crown. Set free upon the earth
By simple gifts of knowing how mere mirth can cut
    the bonds
And pull the blood spikes out;

Their conversation shouts of "Fool!"
That word they teach themselves in every school,
And, having taught, do not like Khayyam's scholars
Go them out by that same door
Where in they went,
But go to rockets through the roofs
To night and stars and space,
A single face turned upward toward all Time,
One flesh, one ecstasy, one peace.

The cross falls into dust, the nails rust on the floor,
The wafers, half bit through, make smiles
On pavements
Where the wind by night comes round
To sit in aisles in booths to listen and confess
I am the dreamer and the doer
I the hearer and the knower
I the giver and the taker
I the sword and wound of sword.
If this be true, then let the sword fall free from hand.
I embrace myself.
I laugh until I weep
And weep until I smile
Then the two of us, murderer and murdered,
Guilty and he who is without guile
Go off to Far Centauri
To leave off losings, and take on winnings,
Erase all mortal ends, give birth to only new beginnings,
In a billion years of morning and a billion years of sleep.

The day burns bright;
The morning, clear,
Has made its way to noon;
And all that seems most special and most dear
Is held encircled by the flaring sun itself.
This weather is for kites
Or earthborne people who
Upon a hill string up their souls
And send them flying in the glare
That brings quick tears to eyes
And warmth to hearts
Which, knowing autumn,
Feel the season change
As birds fly north again
Against the tide of time and time's unreason.
This weather is for children
Or children-men who, melted by the sun,
Find need for toys;
Who stand like boys bedazzled by a sum,
Who thrive on chalking life on hopscotch walks,
Stand here, leap there, run fast, stand very still,
But this now most of all: Be Much Alive.

So in this time of kites,
Autumnal springs, toys, men dwarved small again
In the hot rain
Of sunlight,
Take this string,
Let go with me, let fly the colored paper

On November's wind made March,
And ask with me what color we have flown:
Does Love put up such flags?
And if so, are they white?
Or colored like a hearth gone drowsed and sleepy warm
Deep into night?
Does lust fly high or low?
Some one of us must know;
In chorus, paired, or giving answer
Simple and alone,
Each calling out the color of the kite
Which flies so high on this clear day
Must name his own.

If you will wait just long enough, all goes;
Young woman, if you wait, I'll step away.
O God, it may well take a dozen years,
But finally my tears will dry, my passion wander off
To dust itself in ancient dreams,
My straight loins wither to dried plum,
My words go dumb, adroit excuses for rare matinees
Put unused tickets under pillows,
If you wait long enough, dear one, yes, if you wait
My gait and pace will surely slow.
These are the penalties of age:
That sweet rage dies, that shouts tide down to whispers
And that whispers still themselves in flesh,
That the cogs of love-mad beast no longer even try
     to mesh,
That suddenly long morning sleeps and naps
     in afternoon
Are much preferred to wrestling and to luncheon
     gymnast feats,
That nibbled sweets of thigh no longer seem
The center of the day. They simply idiot-maunder
     off away
Leaving one stunned to wonder and to doubt.
Why shout of jealousy, why envy of another's size?
What prize was that which lay beneath one's chest?
Why wrest such sweetmeats, why that young girl's cries?
Why melt her eyes and yours with happy tears,
Why sighs and cheers and lamentations over endless
     brawls,

Why squalls and calms, then fiercer storms of must,
Why gusts of meat-*machismo,* mask-bravado,
    super-male?
Why flail and torment, doubt: to seed or not to seed?
Why endless need cupped close in need in nest of need?
Sweet Christ, what *was* it all about?

And was it Aristotle who awoke one morn,
Looked down and gave a shout of glad release
And ran to show the servants so they all might see,
The pendant thing hung cold and not aroused,
So down the chamber aisles he cried:
"I'm free! O God, at last, I'm free!"
Well, what a shame.
Or, also, knowing lust, who can blame him?
Yet, oh, it's hard to think that one day all the gods
Will truly pack, depart and leave Olympus in the rain,
That falling down erosions will slide flesh
To ruin in the dusk-lit sea,
As even high gods sink and founder in the soul
And vanish out of sight,
So nights fill now with only dreams,
Remembrance of a time when stallions pissed the air
And brought the mares encircled to their thrust,
When lust was every breath you gave or took,
When earthquakes shook your flanks,
And thrived her blooded subterrane with this and this
    and this!
Again, again, again!

No more.
What *was* all that?

Now you, young woman,
Lovely one curled there, cat-feet tucked under;
Your rare June earth sweet-welcoming this wry
    November's snow,
You, now, you!
What, what, oh, God, oh, what—
(Help me remember!) please!
What's your name . . . ?

The child goes far in worlds within a world,
The girl goes far in green within a green,
That English land where all her blood was born
And rivers run to sea in summers washed by rain
    and sun.
My light and flesh look out her eye aware
And live I in another time and splendid place;
My face somewhat looks lost
And hidden from within her face,
And mingled there, my awe and ingasped worshipping
Do travel far because of her . . .
I visit there with grace,
I know the crossroads of all time,
I wander where the weather is both cold and warm
To wake at nights near Blenheim where the storm
Is like old battles and artilleries drowned deep
In leafage from another year;
I gather flowers by serenities of stream
And touch old stones gone green with velveteens
    of moss,
Soft edge to granite toothings of an ancient dream.
I stay, I go, one flesh is here, the other wanders there,
My older self kept spelled by California airs
My younger, garden-lost in Britain's maze,
But what a joy such days of lostness be!
How wondrous to be lovely-puzzled endlessly!
The sum and thought is good: that even when I stay I go,

Gone quiet here, my other self
Stands even much more silent still,
That one more mystery of myself,
That girl run round the wide circumference of earth
Dares take a step, a step, another step,
And then, behold!
All that was gray at sunset
Mints itself to gold;
All that was cold
Is for a moment, on the hearth of evening, kindled
   warm.
This self, stayed here, calls out a prayer
And asks a promise from the world:
To keep my other lost and wandering self from harm.

Why, damn it all,
You once were *full* of life!
It dripped and fell from off your ruddy edges into Space!
Long years before our time
When dreaming tribes of men lurched in dim caves
And burnt their paws at fires newly made,
They eyed your blazing shape far up the sky
October nights and wondered what you were.
The Greeks, they wondered too,
And so along the line to men who grouped
With Galileo or some-such
Confirmed or dis-established you.
While authors, later on, competed to outfit your
     latitudes
And longitudes with peoples some bleached fair
And others green,
And some with gills, by God, and others saffron gone
     astride
Rare beasts with spider legs;
Some hatched from eggs because dear Mr. Burroughs
     wrote it so!
While others snatched quadruple swords,
One for each arm and hand.
Great gods in multiples, oh what a land you were,
Yes, what a land!
We all of us, as boys, stretched minds in orchestras
     of need,
First one, and then another and another
So, signaling, we hoped that you might mother us,

Pull us like teeth, yank soul from body,
Spirit raw from bloody dreaming flesh
Across the void to land us safe in dust
To run in childish tides among blue hills!
Such thrills were common and from such common stuff
We made up armies of romancers who, full-grown,
Built metal thus to underpin the dreams
And so as astronauts strode forth on fire
And found a moon much less than halfway up to you.
For now, inadequate, 'twill do, oh, yes, 'twill do.
While we save up our spit to make another try
On some day soon this side of century's end,
Put landfall down and self-destruct the dream
That caused us to commence.
Some few days hence we will set out,
        the boys-grown-men
And shuttle us forever back and forth again
Between your far red beacon light
And green and blue and white and mortal Earth.
Our mirth will answer all,
Our laughter in the face of Nothing's smile
Will ring across the abyss mile on light-year mile.
Old Mars, then be a hearth to us some little space
Before we leave your nest to start again a race
That we must win completely or be lost,
And, winning, gain Forever, so not count the cost.
Three billion lights extinguished if one light but stays?
One last light, yes, to touch the fuse and detonate
Three billion unborn men to life, to fire forth

Three billion years of everlasting joys and endless days.
Old Mars, can you help out with this?
Why, can boys piss?
And write their destinies across the skies?
Their names in sand as well as stars?
Oh, yes!
. . . and cross the t's.
. . . and dot the i's.

Night shades a side of me
Which leans unto the North
And calls upon a polar wind to hair my spine
And fills my lungs with dread
That part of me, half-dead,
A left-hand sort of thing gone claw
Is creep and crawler on my bed;
By night I feel my spider hand cup blood
And move of its own itching pride
To throttle up my soul.
Then I have need of sun and my warmed Southern self,
My right hand called from noon
To wrestle with the dark,
To tromp the spidered clutch,
Let loose my soul in brighter gasps of climes
More yellow and more perfect
Than a Savior's exhalations.
So noon and midnight's self cell up in one wild flesh
And own me, each in its own time,
Or turnabout and own me in an instant fused
Where black and white twins mix to make a perfect
    paint
To color out my mask and make a curious sight
Within a mirror's gaze prolong themselves
Half nights, half days.
What man is that? I ask,
Which singer of what song?

And image answers back:
The Thing That Goes By Night:
The Self That Lazes Sun.

Both answers wrong.

What is the Groon?
My young dog said.
What is the Groon;
Is it live, is it dead?
Did it fall from the Moon,
Has it arms, legs, or head?
Does it walk,
Or shamble and amble or stalk?
Does it grumble or mumble or whisper like snow?
Is it dust, is it fluff?
Is it snuff
For a ghost that will sneeze itself inside-out,
Then, outside-in, turnabout!?

Can it walk on the wall?
Will it rise, stay, or fall?
Does it moan, groan, and grieve?
What tracks does it leave
When it walks in the dust
And makes prints by the light,
By the moldy old light of the Moon?

What's the Groon?
Is it he, she, or it?
Does it sprawl, crawl, or sit?
Is it shaped like a craw or a claw or a hoof?
Does it tread like a toad in the road
Or mingle on the shingle-high path
Of our roof?
There, aloof, does it tap in the night

And go down out of sight in the rain-funnel spout?
Is it strange going in,
But even more strange coming out?

Has it shadows to spare?
Is it rare?
Does it croon for a loved one, oh,
Much like itself
Put away on a shelf
In a grave or a tomb
Where it shuttles a loom,
Spins new shapes for itself
Made of moon-moss and lint,
Sparked with Indian flint
Struck from Indian graves
Where old Indian braves
Put their bones up on stilts
Where their mummy-dust silts
Join the corn-stalks in dance;
And the wind off the hills
Chills wild smokes torn from rooves
And the dust churned from hooves
Of ghost horses stormed by
In the middle of night—
What a sight! what a sight!
Is *this*, then, the Groon?

Is it old as the Sphinx?
Is it dreadful, methinks?
Is it Dire, is it Awe?

Does it stick in your craw?
Is it smoke or mere chaff?
Do you whimper or laugh
At this skin of a snake left to blow on the road?
Is it cool-iced hoptoad or deep midnight frog
That goes *Splash!* if you jump?
Does it . . . bump . . . 'neath your bed
Near the head or the toe?
When it's there, *is* it there?
When it's gone, where's it go?

What's the Groon?
Tell me soon . . .
For the Moon's growing older,
And the wind's growing colder,
And the Groon? It grows larger and bolder!
And darker and stranger!
My *soul* is in danger!
For there creep its hands
Twitched from shadowy lands,
Reaching out now to touch
And to hold and to . . . clutch!

Quick, sunlight, bring Noon!
Fight shadows, fight Moon!
Give me morning, bright sun!
Then my battle is won.
For the Groon cannot fight
What is Sun, what is Light!

It will wither away
With the dawn, with the day!
But . . . !
. . . come back . . . next midnight . . .
With its scare . . . and its fright . . .
Once again we will croon:
What's the Groon!

What's . . . the . . . Groon . . . ?

Sometimes, gone late at night,
I would awake and hear
My mother in another year and place
Out walking on the lawn so late
It must have been near dawn yet dark it was
The only light then in the gesture of the stars
Which wheeled around in motionings so soft
They took your breath to see; and there upon the grass
Like ghost with dew-washed feet she was
A maid again, alone, quite singular, so young.
I wept to see her there so strange,
So unrelate to me, so special to herself,
So untouched by the world, so evanescent, free,
With something wild come up in cheeks
And red to lips, and flashing in the eyes;
It frightened me.
Why should she wander out without permit,
Permission saying go or do not go
From us or any other . . . ?
Was she, or My God, wasn't she our mother?
How dare she walk, a virgin, fresh once more
Within a night that hid her face,
How dare displace us in her thoughts and will?!

And sometimes even still, late nights,
I think I hear her soft tread on the sill
And wake to see her cross the lawn
Gone wild with wishing, dreaming, wanting
And crouched down there until dawn,

Washing her hair with wind,
Paying no mind to the cold,
Waiting for some bold strange man
To rise up like the sun
And strike her beauteous-blind!
And weeping I call out to her;
Oh, young girl there,
Oh, sweet girl in the dawn!
I do not mind, no, no.
I do not mind.

Far Rockaway . . .
It seems a state of mind
And not a place.
Is it the Country of the Blind or merely
One more face lost in a fog upon a stretch of sand
That, near the sea, squanders itself in rock
And muffled heartbeats endlessly
Aform, atumble with the crumbled dregs of foam
And murmurings of travel where the wandering
Daft stumbler of the roads gives up and stands,
His shoulder creaked with weights
Of toys left over from a time when he ran out with boys
Who, in the hour, then grossly grew to men,
Have left him for some other roads to town.
So he went out through hills to where
The customs, laws, aims, dreams
And circumventures ran them down
To nothingness
Where fences rusted, rotted and gave way,
Where open fields barked foxes, sang with sparrows
Mocked with crows, accepted snowflakes
In sparse payment for old crimes
Those summers killed, deep buried now, and best forgot
And laid with white.
There, every night, a nightmare rouse and whirl
Of chaff and seed
Snuffed up, is sneezed in four directions;
Thus spent free it flounders, wanders, lingers

Molders deep across the dry and cereal land.
No matter, look, but more than looking, hear:
At starting of the dawn, at spent of dusk,
Beginning or shutting down the storms of year
The paper blowing in a dustboll on the empty road
The seaweed thistling the sand shore shoals
In murmured rustling code which speaks to naught
So Nil gives back a throated trickling of sound:
Far Rockaway.
That Rockaway which Far, which Rocks, which tumbles
      down
The landfall-click-away-along-away
Like time which dusts to ruin and to brine
Down destiny's incline to desert stills,
To ruined clay
Like trollies which excursioned off the cliff
And fell in ticket-punch confettis celebrating dooms
To plunge, to steep, to drown in deeps, and dream of
      summer days
Now in Forever's Keep . . .
As whirlwind dying in your ear lets pollen say
In soughing whistled whining all awhisper
Far
Far
And far beyond far
Rock O rock to sleep in deep night crumbling to night,
To rambled star . . .
Far Rockaway . . .

Across the green of years
A croquet ball comes rolling in the tender moss
To kiss the bright-striped wicket-pole
A kiss of Time.
Through hoops, beneath the shade of trees grown old
When fogs themselves grew tired of their mist
And so turned gray and fell to mold,
Through hoops, the summer sun spins like a globe
Unraveling
Forever circuiting a game
Where players change their faces
Prompt with every thirty years . . .
And shadows of the men upon the lawn
Grow tall at dawn or short again at dusk,
Or, drenched by rain, erased,
Are sketched out by a newer light
As gulls dip down the freshened air with cries
Like beggars gone asouling Harvest Night.

Forever rolls the ball, the wooden round,
Forever waits the wicket to be touched,
Then, ricocheted, the bright stuff spins aback
To start the game again around about;
The toys always the same,
The players always stunned by miracles of doubt.
But yet, for all the seeming lateness of the day,
How rare to find one player who refused to play . . .
We linger here in sun with mallet tender in our hands
    awhile

And all just finished, in the midst, or new begun;
    we smile
Taking or giving the weapon,
Standing aside,
A groom of time or tomorrow's bride,
Retiring to the convent of eternity
Or, rawborn, yelling for some fame
We feel, deserving, waits us on the field in that
    long game.

The tide of players gently rolls,
The ball goes wafted on from each,
The tide subsides but then to rise again
And where the Keeper? and what the Score?
We gaze about, give sums, make calculation
To our secret selves and thus, while never knowing more
Move on, our turfprints denting here and there the green
Until late showers of rain in afternoon
Urge grass to rise and all the faint-made hollows fill,
Gone off down hill we turn upon the scene
To find no trace, no track, no path
Where we have, endless, been.

And from the far side of the field we stand and wave
To others who commence, who breach the day
Assured that it will never end.
A lie? A joyous lie;
To them we cry, we shout,
"By God now, yes! You're right!
    There is no night!

But only dawn and noon
There is no moon!
But only sun and day!"
In silence then we sadden forth our private smiles and
    go our way.

The ball rolls on the whispered grass.
The wicket waits. The hoops resound like harps.
And all the ground of nineteen wondrous years is filled
    with cries:
"Begin! Begin!"
For what is always trembled on beginning
We know now never dies.

What I to apeman
And what then he to me?
I an apeman one day soon will seem to be
To those who, after us, look back from Mars
And they, in turn, mere beasts will seem
To those who reach the stars;
So apemen all, in cave, in frail tract-house,
On Moon, Red Planet, or some other place;
Yet similar dream, same heart, same soul,
Same blood, same face,
Rare beastmen moved to save and place their pyres
From cavern mouth to world to interstellar fires.
We are the all, the universe, the one,
As such our fragile destiny is only now begun.
Our dreams then, are they grand or mad, depraved?
Do we say yes to Kazantzakis whose wild soul said:
God cries out to be saved?
Well then, we go to save Him, that seems sure,
With flesh and bone not strong, and heart not pure,
All maze and paradox our blood,
More lost than found,
We go to marry stranger flesh on some far burial ground
Where yet we will survive and, laughing, look on back
To where we started on a blind and frightful track
But made it through, and for no reason
Save it must be made, to rest us under trees
On planets in such galaxies as toss and lean
A most peculiar shade,

And sleep awhile, for some few million years,
To rise again, fresh washed in vernal rain
That is our Eden's spring once promised,
Now repromised, to bring Lazarus
And our abiding legions forth,
Stoke new lamps with ancient funeral loam
To light cold abyss hearths for astronauts to hie
    them home
On highways vast and long and broad,
Thus saving what? Who'll say salvation's sum?
Why, thee and me, and they and them, and us
    and we . . .
And God.

Strange grief, grand joy, remember? Once a foolish year
We gathered in some old gymnasium
That smelled of sweaty seas that dried to dust;
There sexual exercisers, going gray,
Came them to table
With their sons, not yet, yet hopeful, after lust,
And sat in twins along the white and silver way
To eat back chicken and sad peas
And drifts of long-departed winter snows,
Those sweltered and destroyed-by-summer-night
     ice creams.
Then strangely for one moment in it all,
Someone said something that was *right*.
And each sat tall up in his flesh and knew his bones
And none knew whether he was boy or man,
Son or father of the son;
When all was Team,
Found twin.
Suddenly bemused, befuddled and befogged by tears,
By love surprised, expressed,
Only to be lost a second later
When, hands unclasped, shoulders unhugged,
Clean ears unkissed, brows uncaressed, all bent them
     once again
To the untouchable flavors of swiftly melting time.
The scheme that was divined into the light
Sinks now again in yarns of numb spaghetti
Never to be unknit by rhetoric.
So, unspun, the dream retreats

To its dumb and brute-bone hiding place
As tears salt-dry the cheeks, start back in stunned
And blinded eyes
And leave no trace.

Remembering all this last night,
I saw my father stride within a memory film
Which ran the length of me
But measured *him!*
Behind my flesh in amiable disguise
I found him lurked in my not-knowing
But now seeing and appraising eyes.
He long has slept away to moss.
All the more reason then for my sad searching
And my sense of loss.
For he is hardly here in nose or jaw or ear.
But, ah, look! There! atumble in the hair on wrist and arm
Like glints of gold and amber and bright sun,
There everything I was and am and will be soon
Deep run.
O, sometimes twice a day I catch him treading by!
Or, if alert with only simmers of half-vision
On the flexed wide sill of patient eye,
Some dozen times or more, especially at noon,
I capture him in fry and burn and brazen heat;
He lifts my hands to catch a phantom ball,
He runs my feet to hurdles that fell down
And ruins stayed some forty years ago.
I plan to catch him so, in shocks, abrupt entrapments,

Rare delights,
A hundred thousand times or more before I die.
My dad, old pa, that loving father there
Awrestle in bright sweat,
All nestled in the clockspring copper twine
That furs me with a sunset fire
And speaks with light and tells more with a silence
Than my lost sad soul can half divine.
He rambles where the ants of childhood scurried on my
    knuckles,
Now lost, now found, he waves for me to see him
On that most strange hearth, my wheat-field arm,
My whorled palm and fingertip, my harvest flesh.
Dear God, praise Him, that He connives,
That He burns wide my gaze with *both* these lives:
To see the father in the son all snug
And tucked and warm and happy-fine inside.
Miraculous! that pore and blood
And cell and gene and chromosome
Are that odd immortality we rarely note or speak of
For a home.
Yet home it is, and threshold of the fire
Where father, playing at a death
Did sink, retire, and stoke him up a warmer blaze:
Myself . . . a bon rekindled with genetic praise.
His fingers hover as I hover out my grasp,
My breath of exultation, thanking Providence,
Sighs out a prayer with every gasp.
Thankful for me, I give my thanks to him,

In twin thanksgivings then we share our single heart
    with grace,
And love this soul, this flesh, these limbs,
Our basking place.
We are the stuff of each other's dreams;
He the long since melted and vanished
And I all that remains of those dimly remembered
Warm June summer night ice creams . . .

And now at last
From the long lazing drowsy fathers and sons banquet of life
We wander home
Two on the same sidewalk
Ambling as one.
And still tonight, tonight,
Alone and shaving, the rippled mirror bright,
My own gaze seeks beyond this lather-mask and foam;
Old One, I miss but find you here,
This is your home
And yours my marrow
And I your son.
Never were there two of us but only one.
Once the one was you.
But with the changings of the sea
The tide, gone out, returns,
And now, now, now, O, now . . .
. . . that one is me.

Sweetest love, come now to meet me,
Touch your solitude to mine;
Take, enfold, protect and greet me,
Save me from my world with thine.
Give me more than I might borrow,
Much of joy, yet some of sorrow;
Search and find in Love's high attics
Horizontal mathematics,
Toys to prove the simple sums
That honeys, nectars, pollens, gums
Of Love's taking, giving, grieving,
Sweetly seeding and conceiving
Will thrive our days to myth and lore:
Two separate minds, one flesh the score.

Deftly sing it, lady, praise
How I lose me in your maze,
Gladly lost there, never found,
In your honeyed underground.
People asking then for me,
Tell them where I buried be.
Tangled in your private wild,
Say that you grow large with child,
So one day from secret earth
Middle age will find rebirth.
I not to tomb, but hence to womb
Where your maidenhair then growing

Clothes this ancient peach afresh,
Robes it round with April flesh.

O, men by thousands, such as I
Would gladly 'neath your sweet grass lie
To claim what's tucked beneath your lawn
Will rise as fresh and young as dawn.

Love's Time Machine will shelve me there
And chaff the old to new and fair
And, nurtured, kept, by nectars mild
Be born again as your last child.

God is a Child;
Put toys in the tomb
And He will come play.
What's new in this?
Why, not a thing at all.
It was known and tried
So many years upon a year ago,
When kings knew swift-lost sons
Who went to dust in summers
That turned wintry chill
Within a night.
All humble-proud, those captain kings departed
To the tomb
And there by still sarcophagi of amiable sons gone cold
And rambled off across the abyss rim
Astroll upon the meadows of parched space,
The weeping monarchs set down toys
That only yestermorn were in the hands of child.
These fragments of lost play,
Strewn all about like breadcrumbs for some mighty bird
To come and pluck and eat,
Were thus left there
In hopes that God or gods, a singular or plural Presence
Might, paused curious, see,
And step in across the mortal sill
To spend a while each night in splendid joyful wakes
By sleeping son;

To nudge his stuffs, to wake his soul perhaps;
So boy and God might squat awhile
On tombstone floor and rattle numbered bones
Or tremble ghostly xylophones and shiver harps
Or trace in dust a hopscotch pentagram
And dive in it
To swim on river tides of moon
Let down through windows of the vault.
Could God refuse such sport?
No, no. Our God, Forever's Child,
Will always play and show rambunctious wills
Among the molecules and atom storms
As well as knockabout of toys within a silent
    dungeon keep.
Let the world sleep.
Let father sit outside the door
And only now and then peek in at toys
Placed there about the box where his son hides;
And if he hears twin laughters,
One seedling-sparrow small,
The other vast as weathers off the sea,
Let him not look at all
But weep, and turn his tears to joys
That there, hid down, asprawl in floury gusts
    of midnight tomb,
There be a frolic of brothers/fathers/sons . . .
Oh listen! Let the sound fill up your heart!
That tumult of the large
And oh so pitifully weak small happy boys.

Ben Franklin was that rarity:
A man whose jolly-grim polarities did tempt our God
To hurl his bolts which, fastened to Ben's ears,
Lit up his cerebrum for years
And thus illuminated reams of history.
His dreams, electric dreams,
Were knocked together out of Boy Mechanic schemes;
He wet his finger, held it to God's Mystery and Storm.
God, in turnabout, gesticulated, touched
To know Ben's warm or cooling weather.
So somehow these unconvivial two
Fell in together and were friends.
Their means quite different
But most similar-same their ends:
To Light the Universe,
Or light a world,
Large thing or small.
God blinked and Lo! the Nebulae!
Ben blinked; electric founts poured from his hands;
Within a century his sparks had lit the lands
And filled the towns with noon at night.
Such was God's vision.
Such was Ben's sight.
And after long years, some eighty-odd or more
Of intemperate days, good afternoons, storms, calms,
Bad fights, then making peace,
Vast multiples of weather,
God yawned, Ben gummed his eyes,
But still arguing . . . went off to bed together.

Some live like Lazarus
In a tomb of life and come forth curious late
To twilight hospital and mortuary room.

From one womb to another
Is but a falling step;
Yet Innocence unbandaged
Blinks at Truth in terror
And would blind itself again!

But better the lame drags forth at last
From morning sickness waxed to twilight sleeps
Thine own self litter forth in autumn's self-consume
Than linger in one room.

Let summer wander idiot in these eyes
Which stricken wide one wild sweet moment upon day
Fix, transfix, and die,
Than, warned by widows, stifled in a cage
All stillborn stay.

From first cry to last breath
If all one knows is death upon a frost-rimed path
To yet more ice,
Let one warm breath suffice
For July dawns of hail
And August snows when stormbound senses fail.

Best Lazarus born of witch-hag, shocked, miscarrying
Than, senses shorn, gone ill with thought

Of marrying ear to music,
Eye to luscious color,
Nose to time and tide's caprice,
Hand to squalor.
Tongue to late sour wine must answer sweet.
Mere roadway dust-track now name street.

Best Lazarus born a dwarf dismembered
Than cat-sick hairball choked in half-out,
Hid moth-hair, chaff-seed, cold steam of un-lust
Unthrust, by hungry Death himself quite ill-remembered,
Never birthed at all.

Better cold skies seen bitter to the North
Than blind unseeing sac-bile gone to ghost.
If Rio is lost, love the Antarctic Coast.
O ancient Lazarus!!
Come ye forth.

The ladies in the libraries
Do not go home at night;
Stand watch, be sure, just wait
Outside the mellow place at nine
Crouched down in bush and elderberry vine,
Look in through windows tall
Where virgin brides go quiet as the dust
By shelves where titles ranked, gold-bright as foxes' eyes,
Glint sparks of lust.
Among the million dead and million more to perish
These unsparked flints, these uncut gravestone brides
Do nourish silence, and their tread
Is stuff of moss and downfell rust.
They do not touch the floor, incircling the dark,
To one-by-one pull strings to snatch the light,
Extinguish and move on to next and snatch again,
Keys at their waists ajingle in a gentle rain,
Like skaters in a summer dream,
Their spectacles agleam beneath the greenglass shades.
The smell of hyacinth pervades where they have been
And goes before as harbinger of youngness kept
Clasp-corseted in Iron Maiden flesh.
Where air was warm and bounteous on the sill,
In passing, such as these give vapors and the chill
To airs that touch and move aside.
They hide themselves a moment in the stacks
To shove long needles murderous in their hair
And find themselves in mirrors, unaware;

Both seer and seen the Queen of Iceland's crop,
A blind stare, a strange drift of unshaped snow.
Then, at the door they go, give last looks round the
   shop
Where Time is vended in the books,
Where skin prolapses from the dinosaur,
Then wheel again to knife the air, go out and down
   the street
To places no one knows.
They do not go.
Their coats all buttoned tight,
Their spectacles fresh-washed, they spin to call:
"Is anybody there?"
In hopes that some deep terrifying voice of man
Might some night soon reply, "Ah, yes."

Their ringless fingers tremble on their dress.
They hold their breath, their souls, they wait.
Then reach up for the last light-string and yank.
The night drops down.
But in the instant of eclipse
They snap-close-clench themselves like
Ancient paper flowers of Japan.
A wind from basements dank and attics desert-dry
Breathes up, breathes down the air,
These scentless flowers shower everywhere!
And where before the brittle women stood,
Some vagrant tattered crepes now tap the floor.
As for the rest, the lustful books on shelves gape wide

And into these the funeral-flower souls now rattle,
Tickle, rustle, hide, and, hiding, rest;
Each to its age, each to its own and proper nest.
This maid to Greece and Rape of the Sabines,
That one to Child's Crusade
Where knights shuck off their stuffs
To bed the sixteenth summer maid;
The third and last cold statue turned to farewell
    summer's dust
Flies up the Transylvania height
And welcomes lust by showing it her neck
And trading randy bite for bite.
All, all turned to bookmarks! Slipped in dreadful books
Where loving makes a din
Ten times as loud as loving in the world beyond the
    shelves.
Tucked in warm dark the bookmark maidens
Feel themselves crushed and beauteously mangled,
Scream and gibber all the night,
Only swooning down to dreaming sleep at dawn,
Smiles creped about their mouths.
Squashed flat 'twixt Robin and his nimble nibbling men,
And Arthur who, if thanked,
Will pull Excalibur from them at breakfast-time,
And so be King, his weapon free of stone
That held it fast, all hungry for a fight.

Such screams! Such gladsome mourns of happiness!
List, listen! by the library.

But, soft . . . the books, gummed shut, do muffle it.
The maids all night each night are maids no more.
Come back at noon.
And see the ancient cronies three, aswoon,
All somewhat tipsy-drunk and tenterhooked with memory
Propped up at desks as if the sun were still the moon.
Give nod,
Give book,
Go off, but never ask, for you will never know
Where, where o where at night
These long lost cold-chipped marble ladies go.
Ask silence,
Linger on awhile
But all you'll have for answer
Is a sad remembrance smile
They'll quickly cover with a Kleenex, wipe away.

So, old again and lonely and unsquashed
And ringless, pale, and breathing only ice,
They face the heatless noon,
The sunless hours of day,
Reckon your question,
Recommend files,
And give virginal advice.

The truth is this:
That long ago in times
Before the birth of Light,
Old Dante Alighieri prowled this way
On continent unknown to mad Columbus;
Made landfall here by sneaking, sly Machine,
Invention of his candle-flickered soul
Which, wafted upon storms,
Brought him in harmful mission down.
So, landed upon wilderness of dust
Where buffaloes stamped forth
A panic of immense heartbeat,
Dante scanned round and stamped his foot,
And hoofed the trembling flints
And named a Ring of Hell.
With parchment clenched in tremorous fist,
He inked out battlements of grime
And arcs of grinding coggeries which, struck,
Snowed down a dreadful cereal of rust
Long years before such iron soots were dreamt
Or made, or flown,
Long long before such avenues of steel in sky were
    sought.
So, in a guise like Piranesi lost amidst-among
His terrible proud Prisons,
The Poet sketched a vaster, higher, darker Pent-up Place
A living demon-clouded sulphur-spread of Deep.
From tenement to tenement of clapboard dinge
He rinsed a sky with coal-sack burning,

Hung clouds with charcoal flags
Of nightgowns flapping like strange bats
Shocked down from melancholy steam-purged
    locomotive caves.
Then through it all put scream of metal flesh,
Great dinosaur machines charged forth by night,
All stomaching of insucked souls
Pent up in windowed cells.
Delivered into concrete river-shallow streets,
Men fled themselves from spindrift shade
Of blown black chimney sifts and blinds of smoking
    ghosts.
And on the brows of all pale citizens therein
Stamped looks of purest terror,
Club-foot panic and despair,
A rank, a raveling dismay that spread in floods
To drain off in a lake long since gone sour
With discharged outpouring of slime.

So drawn, so put to parchment, so laid down
In raw detail, this Ring of Hell (No mind what Number!)
Was Dante's greatest Inventory counting-up
Of Souls in dread Purgation.
He stood a moment longer in the dust.
He let the frightened drumpound heart of buffalo tread
Please to excite his blood.
Then, desecration-proud, happy at the great Black Toy
He'd printed, builded, wound, and set to run
In fouled self-circlings,

Old Dante hoisted up his heels,
Left low the continental lake shore cloven, stamped,
And hied him home to Florence and his bed,
And laid him down still dreaming with a smile,
And in his sleep spoke centuries before its birth
The Name of this Abyss, the Pit, the Ring of Hell
He had machinery-made:

CHICAGO!

Then slept,
And forgot his child.

They say you cannot, no, in any way
Go home again.
Yet home I came,
And picked an hour when the train
Slid in upon the golden track of twilight to the town.
I rode in bronze and saw the panoply of ore
Laid out on every leaf and every roofing cope
And balustrade;
The train rode high on trestle as it braked on toward
    its stop
And I gazed out upon that special dusking sea
Which washes for scant minutes on the world
At rise and set of sun.
Stepped down, I moved upon the yellow planks
Torn up from all the halls of ancient myths.
The station sign was gold.
The trees, my god, the trees wore epaulettes!
The ivy on the old school wall was dazzling braid.
And in the shade the eye of cat sent forth
A minted signaling which could be spent!
The walks I trod were saffron from an Indian sand;
The lawns were amber carpetings
Where warrior ants climbed stricken with such
    luscious tints
As made them seem the richest armory in time.
Mere bees upon the air were tapestries.
And down the slanted beams of now-lost afternoon
And soon-come night
A spider made his way

On harps of honey-colored twine
Which struck might cry with pure delight.
All, all was light!
The very air swam syrupy with tunes of wind
And rattlings of coins which tufted every branch.
The leaves beneath each tree were jackpot avalanche.
A dog trot-rambled by
His fur made up of stuffs from out Fort Knox,
His eyes cuff-links he sported without pride,
Accepted, knew, forgot, and took in stride.
The house where I was born,
My grandma's house,
Most terrible, most beautiful of all!
As I came by
Aflame it was, all fire in the windows
From the plunging sun;
Each glass a meld of brazen metals
From old shields on which a thousand dead
Were proudly borne toward sunset cairns.
As if raised high upon the instant of my coming
The windows dazzled, clamoring the lawns,
Then rushed to set more torches
On the blazing rose-filled porches,
And attics danced with firefly dust
As cupolas took light like lust
And virgin chandeliers were crazed
And cracked with flame.
I stood amazed,
I trod the flaxen grass;

Let smoldering towers blind my gaze.
Never such welcome!
In all my days of going forth and coming back,
Never such wealth.
The sunset knew my lack
And sparked a million bons to show the way,
All celebrant, a burning down of happiness
Before my river-running, gladsome-fractured eyes.
All of its banks it opened,
All of its wealth it spent
In one last great pervading spree.
I sensed but one cool shade of Death behind
    a single tree
Waiting for the silent river of light to ebb
So it might seize not only cash but me.
But now it was an hour all sweetly met;
I did come home and chose by clumsy miracle
A time which made the world stand still
Mute-struck to bronze.
A statue, then, I fed myself the splendid prides of air
And heard the birds that sang with jeweled throats:
You'll live forever. This, your summer, gone eternal,
Will stay fair.
I stayed.
The sun went out.
The sky shut down its light.
Gone wise, a few days later, rising up near dawn
I made my way through streets of night
To train and left the way I came—

As sun fired gold to mint the town;
Still the same king I was upon arriving
All royal gowned I left in a lie of light.
The last I saw of it
The town was, avenue and shop, bright swathed
In goldleaf touching and renewed.
A tree all dripped with Spanish royal doubloons
Shook with premonitions as I passed
And mouthed farewells.

In Chicago
Some hours later,
The railway station men's room
Smelled like the lion house
At the zoo
In Dublin
When I was very old.

And dark our celebration was,
For Death was sweet to us;
By that I mean it filled our sacks so full
We leaned atilt round moonlit corners of the town
And sprinted on to doorways where we buzzed and rang
And lit the pumpkin windows and held forth our hands
To take the treasures of the time,
Then ran again, my lovely thistle girls and I
Gone old within a night yet young with them.

How grand such Eves, how good such girls
That they slowed pace for ancient boys like me.
Who could not give it up, stay home, put by that holiday.
I had to go, to lurch, to tap, to laugh, to walk at last
All happy-tired home in cold wind blowing
With the full-lit moon to wife and hearth and aunts
Come by to wait for us: the crazy man and his wild pride
Of maiden beasts.
Long years ahead, dear girls, on nights like those,
Do please drop by at dusk, come sit upon my stone
And speak glad words
To spirit gone but wishing to be still
With you when you go forth with your own children
Thus to filch and prize and laugh at every door.
No more. I stay.
But save for me a single sweet, some Milky Way
    to munch

Or bring a pumpkin cut and lit and place it so to warm
    my feet.
Then on the path run, go! knowing that I'm not dead,
For you are my head, my heart, my limbs, my blood
    set free;
You are the me that is warm,
I am the me that is cold,
You are the me that is young,
I old.
But what of that?!
Death's mean at all his Tricks, God, yes,
But you the Treats
Who run to beg my life and yours
In all the Future's wild, delirious, dark
But warm and living streets.

And did you know that still she was alive?
Somewhere, old Harriet Hadden Atwood, there's a name!
And freshly gone now at, listen to the sum:
One hundred years plus five!
Why, gods in multiples, there's no one else alive
Recalls what she recalled just some few days ago
When in her bed, remembering, she tuned pianos past
    our ken;
She outlived twenty-on-a-thousand better men
And women who shored up their bones
And lived out lives on borrowed blood
And loans of vital stuffs,
While kindling up her dreams with echoings of song
That needle-hissed her mind all midnight long.
She played for Edison!
Old Thomas asked her talent to begin.
So she began and in beginning knew no end.
George Atwood came to find her at Old But Then Young
    Edison's request.
Timidly she came, all doubt, and saw the strange
    machine
In which he would entrap, wind up her trembled soul,
There nest her sound like fragile mail
To be delivered in some unfrequented year
She would frequent by song and song alone,
Her body gone, her touch would linger on the sill
And fill the year Two Thousand Ninety-Nine with chords.
Her late rewards?
A tumult of applause broadcast down shoals of stars

And Space
From all the future places where the race
Has gone, will go, to hide and seek,
The billions of them nameless as they go.
But, strange—
The name of Harriet Hadden Atwood they will know.

For Edison she played.
This maid another year did sit her down
In some small glade of time
And place her fingers to the keys
From which sprang old but now-made-new within-the-
    instant
Melodies.
Her claims were modest,
Nor did she take a fee
She removed her gloves and gently kicked the pedals
A trimly perfect mediocrity—
Which means not bad nor yet a hair beyond
The median good;
She was a known commodity in the tuneless humming
    of bees
That was her green-fern, sharp-thorned summer rose
And cut-grass neighborhood.
All children, with their butterflies like Fates
Caught up in nets, nodded as she passed,
Their fingers aching at remembrance of strict lessons
That she taught;

She baked and bought the simples of her Time.
When in between a lesson or recital
Less than humble are her vital statistics,
Less than a complication the logistics of supply
    and demand
In her life.
Tom Edison needed a sweet-sour pound of high green
    summer apples;
George Atwood looked and found: a pianist, then
    a wife.
Both were gladdened by her sound.
Now that sound will gladden out the hearts of girls
    unborn
Beyond Poughkeepsie, Saturn, Jupiter,
Far Rockaway, Moon, Mars, or Matterhorn.
In nebulae at present kept beyond our gaze
Harriet Hadden Atwood, who played for the
    now-long-dead
In other days,
Will, in future ages,
Doubtless in Alpha Centauri,
Be counted as one of their new and unpredictable
    culture rages.

Unknown in her own time,
No titan talent she.
Yet since she was the start of some new thing,
One billion years from tonight

She will bloom in eternal spring.
Five light-years away and away,
Miss Maiden-Lady Hadden, later found-and-married
    Atwood,
Will play and play and play.
Tom Edison asks it!
In séance he sets her task ever on:
More, yes! once more, yes, now, more!
Five presidents heard and sent notes
On her birthdays recalling some raggedy tunes
They'd last heard on some late summer night
Now-gone-forever excursion boats.
Such threadbare keys,
By a passaging of time beyond the lees of every planet
In our basement system of the Void
May well outlive the off-beat hummings of a Freud,
Linger with Beethoven,
Stay with Berlioz.
Made up of humble clay,
Harriet Hadden Atwood, a girl whose only Cause
Was to play
Piano
Trapped by Thomas Alva E.,
Now lives Forever!
Give or take a day.

All things are mixed.
The very flesh of God
Is compound eye which looks upon a world
And cracks the light,
And fixes star at very blackest heart of night,
And shades the noon with ghost
And leans the shadow tree
Across the flowered lawn,
And fringes, all serene,
The sea with teeth of carnivore
Which boil in hungry schools beneath the calms;
What seems a balm is salt to ancient wounds;
What seems a death, gone teeming unto worms,
From splendid garbage rouses up new forms;
Beneath the mask of Peace
Old War hones swords and builds
A battlement of scrimshaw bone;
Beneath the battered shield
Soft flesh, gone simple with a summer's day,
But waits for asking and then, asked, gives yield.
So round-about all goes, now hard, now soft,
Now mild, now mad, the sheep and wolf arun in tandem
    flocks:
Lost man, found world,
Fused paradox.

The sky is inked with blue
The grass, sketched, scribbled, drawn, is green ink, too,
And all about ravines take children to their Deeps;
While from the east at dawn and west at sunset seeps
A color of life's blood
Where clouds amass
And spread the tincture.
At the airport, dragon-shadows pass,
Kites shuttle
Shadow down
Becoming planes
Which
Oh
So
Softly
Land
On . . .
. . . grass.

On rooftops roosters cut from metal
Whine with wind and nose gone-far directions
Where only children with their secret
Gum-chewed mint impacted wisdom go.
The eaves glide-whisper soft of summer nights
Now letting flow
The silk discumberments of dreams:
Remembered snow.

Rivers run here not filled with summer dust
Or sun-crazed rock and idiot stone

But actual water.
At noon the streets are church-nave deep in cool
    green shade
Across the lawns: battalions of glare,
Sun-dandelions
Clock-light the drifting grin and footpad ease of dog,
The vacuum-cleaner exhaled dust-fluff cat,
The rubber tread of never-silent boy.

Here all beautifully collides
Unfrictioned;
Summer heals all with an oiled and motioned ease.
Here no disease.
Here health of world in distilled proportion,
Here gyroscope ahum kept spun by bees
Who drowse-drown lusciously entrapped by flowers
Or hummingbirds which fatten forth the hours with pure
    dripped sound . . .
In libraries where dry flowers drop
From books of printed flowers
Old clocks run dry of time keep rigid frozen pointed
At never known, so never remembered, so never
    forgotten, hours.
The librarian has been there forever.
She was never young;
But will seem younger as we grow years.
The stamping of the purple inkstamped data in the books
Is like the tread of wisdom in this place;
The lily-pages blow and whisper
Boys go lost and murmuring in the stacks

Where all is mystery of green-mossed well
Where ignorance shouts to hear a learning echo.
These be the granite cliffs and quarries where we swim
In cooling words on summer midnights
And come forth printed o'er with poems
Which toweled from our flesh yet drip from fingertips
And stifle up the eyes with most sad joys.

All, all town, home, shop, Elite Theatre, library:
    first class.
A first class summer in a first class town.
Where green ink skies make green rains fall, enfilter down.
While at the airport,
Oh, God, look!
How soft,
How sweet and rolling,
See! They pass! All dragon-shadow!
The kited planes
Strings cut,
Laze . . .
. . . drifting . . .
Down . . .
To land . . .
On
Grass.

What's rough is this:
That life, which was a building up of bricks
From which one piped one's exultations,
Now crusts itself within,
The nested stuff keeps soot,
So every cell upon a cell is darkened
With accumulant small dooms,
Some deft disasters of those lesser morns
Which were forgot by noon
But now in numbers rank themselves
And by their very armies overwhelm.
The spirit suffers at the count,
The soul is smothered by their waves.
One's laughter is stopped up and jugged
Within the boneyard cage of rib;
One wants to shout these damned molecules away,
With single rear-backed roars and declamation
Give jolt and pound and hammering of chimney bricks
So all the soot falls down, an evil snow,
And life and flesh and soul gust up,
Are cleansed to joy themselves again
And morns are sweet when one wakes up
And feels a boy stir over, hid within
And turned all smiling to hear cries
Of other boys, all juiced with sun and desperate below
Tossing soft light pebble laughter up to rap
The ice-clear window panes
Till life runs out to meet

Before the body joins
The soul on summer paths to drowning wilderness.

O, God, give strength to those like me
Who in their middle years so dearly wish
To pay with laughs the lurking Dustman
That most strange Chimney Sweep,
So he might knock this hearthing place
This frame of brittling skeleton
And wash all back to rinsed pink brick again,
Restart the fires
And dampen not their ardor
Yet a while.
I would stand baked in my own blood
Warm hands with self's hid fiery surprise,
A fire in each cell and all cells swarmed
With the vast true sun's uprise.

But how knock soot, clean dirt away
Which blinds the soul to its own lineaments,
Which tamps the ears so one can miss
The rare teakettle simmer of warm breath
From out one's grateful mouth?

For Christmas then, O God, kick me a holy kick
Of great outcharged delight.
Gone midnight with too many dusks

And dawns of knowledge,
Knock me white,
O God, yes do!
Strike me with laughter's downflashed lightning;
Make me Light!

O, tell me not, dear Will,
That cowards die a thousand deaths;
I know, I know!
Why every breath I take does crack my bones,
Tear my flesh asunder,
Undermine my mask with moans and sighs.
And yet, while full of death and lies,
More full of pomegranate life and truth this coward be;
I am reborn, O Jesus' nailed and frightened breath, why,
    hourly.
And with such mirth!
Why, listen,
Even though my shocked eyes burn and glisten
With tears torn free by griefs and mad surprise,
What cries of joy, also!
At the crazed and awful triumph up from Death,
Again and again and again I cull in breath
With equal seizures of fright,
Shout back the night, call in the morn,
Thus being reborn and, O much thanks! reborn.

And all of ye brave
Who die but once?
Get you to the grave.
For you dumb remain, and go all mute to mounds and
    worms.
My terms for life are better,
For while brother to night and dying each hour,
I, seeded with terror and handsome dread,

Am rebirthed as funeral flower
Which speaks again and, with panics of heart's lost
    blood, again.

Your panoply of Will is steel which keeps out pain and
    thought,
From which you cannot speak.
My life is dearly bought;
I strike from shadows some few flints of light
While strickened is my heart
And flesh so thin to wounds it bleeds me white.
Yours is the bravery of fools
That will not last the night;
Death and the tomb your wit, your law,
Your first and final Rite.
Ride high in pomp, strut, drum, and flutter flags,
And go to Doom all bound up brave.
Your destiny is dumb.
Long after dark, *my* tongue will writhe
Like sunset snake within my grave
To prove that cowards do speak best and true and well.
And trumpeters and drummers of bravado, *they* . . . ?
Go to Hell.
Go to Hell.

At night she came within my room
All breathing out of weather kept from Time . . .
A summer here, a summer there,
Spent days, warm haze and blue delights,
Remnants of some spun-toy winter nights,
A sound of sleds that rocked the sleep of worlds.
A tinsel cry of icicle on upper tower keep
A sound of wakening
A sound of sleep,
All these, transistorized
Packed in the cells and whorls
And thumbprints of her hum-spun spirit glass
Then caused her Ouija hand to move
And write in quiet motions large my name and Fate
Upon the loving dark over my bed.
Yes! Yes! to all I asked she said,
And firmly No when No was needed.
This woman warm as breast of slumbering fowl,
With wisdom seeded,
Kept safe my years and lanced my most infectious tears
With careful hand or handkerchief,
And held me close to smell her secret whispering
And murmuring machines,
The armory of electric creatures which
With echoings of kites on high March days
Said, "Boy, you'll live forever. Go in peace . . . "
Then went I, running,
Tom, from my electric Gran.
And now when grown into a man

I look me back and see her all aglow in dark,
Her mind a circuitry,
Her veins pale tapestries of spark,
Her hair full panoplied with light
A dim torch wavering of Liberty by night
Electric hive of wisdom from which bees
Lit forth and stung me to my chores . . .
A library, a toyshop vault, a keep of wisdom's spores;
Where centuries of freshly dusted gray philosophers
Wake from sleep
And speak out of her mouth
And from her tongue
Use her for bell and clapper
And there all clung and hung upon a lightning tower
They announce the Past, an amiable present,
And some future hour sung of in banged voices
    from the bell,
Here Schopenhauer gives shout,
There Dante trudges Hell.
Sweet Gran, electric Grandma of my life
You keep in minuscule a.c.–d.c. dungeons deep
The poets of an Age, a deaf-mute Sage perhaps
Who speaks but from your eyes
And cavemen also from a time of brute surmise
All these are shadow-painted on your brow
And throng your pomegranate soul
In which I burrowed like the monkey-mole
Now leapt akimbo, now thrusting sod
Now nosing Devil and now vaulting God.

O grandmother of years,
O mother of the mineral soils of Earth,
I see you wandered on the midnight lawn,
A stillness kept, a waiting to begin.
A woman? No. A pageantry of wheels?
Much more.
A tin soul, trapped and mouthed, which felt the Universe
And spoke its mysteries at dawn.

Boys are always running somewhere.
Ask them where, in running, they all go?
They'll prance around, dance backward,
Answer, puzzled:
They don't know.
And with a glance that says you're sad or mad
     for asking,
On they'll flow.
They are a river-run of Time;
Theirs not to ask or answer but to fit
The rhyme of circumstance and old beginnings
     without end;
God sends them forth for His own Reasonings
To south-east-north or why not west?
Whichever's first is best.
Whichever's second, well, that's second-rate,
But better to be second, moved, in motion
Than be late for beckonings of Fate and rare fell plights
That wait beyond horizons, atop hills,
Fired by dawns,
Or gone acold in dreadful deep November nights.

Boys are always running somewhere.
Not to start is a sin.
Who's to say they should not leap from bed,
Roar from house, chockful of hotcakes, rituals and rites,
Ever ready to begin?

Men are always running somewhere.
Ask them on the train, the jet, the rushing sidewalk, where?

They'll shift their suitcase or their gum
Or their cigar,
To ponder, wonder, peer, then, shut up, wander off,
Thinking you even madder and somehow sadder
Than the boys who thought you mad and sad,
And thus immunized to joys.

Twelve years before,
If boys were all yearning,
Now, as men, they have been to where they wanted
    to run,
Reached the end of the line, had their tickets
    punched
And circle back again
With tossed confetti-stuffs on hatbrim and lapel
To prove their madcap learning,
To show wherever it was, was a party!
And what the hell.
But, brushing the unknown Mardi Gras from off their
    eyebrows,
Hefting their great-coats stuffed with memos,
Ask them now not where they're going
But where've they *Been?*
They'll cudgel up their brows and scowl
As if some survey-maker had just been delicately
    obscene,
Recheck their datebooks, shuffle
Maunder,
But not spell those Destinations Past . . .
They've Gone! So what's to tell?

Going was all the custom.
Now the custom is: Having Been.

And you?
Standing there with your battered kite and no string?
It's obvious you've never went or gone
Or made the scene or, trying, failed,
Or done a thing!
You go not barefoot,
Neither are you shod by Mercury, Apollo,
Or any other plain or fancy god.

Where were they going?
Where last seen?
The man and boy stand tall and small before you;
One gray, the other green,
And, damn it! cry:
They've been Far Traveling . . .
Boy running to meet the man,
Man running to meet the boy,
Collision-course; struck bruised,
All tender-fused, why, look!
They make a troop,
A regiment of two
Who ramble thus forever in their single, simple,
Rare rambunctious joy.

So, suddenly, we see
Where the one was wandering, what he wanted to be;
Where the other has been and, having been, will forever know.

Ask, yes, but answers are absurd.
Like dogs they'll stand and cock their heads at you
And tell no word.
But looks can say:
"I ran to be the man."
Or, "Once I was a boy in summer, rushing to be me."
It is no sin to not know where you've come from,
Or where go. Why should they tell,
When at their secret hearts they spell
The finest truths, and, spelling, mow the lawns of summer,
Barking, snapping, circling, biting, yapping,
There they vault, sunsets
There they share dawns.
There, ambidextrous to delight, they flow.
And who's to stop that joy which hides and seeks
Like child in man?
And who's to warn and tell, prevent,
The man who calls out to the boy?
Here lie their tandem prints in blowing sands—
Quick! here they turn back!
To wipe out their prints with a smile, a shout,
With quick paws that are hands.

Boys are always running somewhere.
Where, where, where O where?
They know.
Men are always running running running somewhere.
O woman, woman of all the sad wise years,
Let them go.

O to be a boy in a belfry
Tilting summer noon in tumults,
On your back, the sun squeezed lemon in your eyes,
The blue heaven all bright fries,
Your feet raw naked to the light,
Strewn warm in bed of straw high up in tower
And this your hour to summon all to prayer.
An incense burns the wind,
The altars wait to tremble,
The ancient dust to tingle
As you kick heel and toe,
Strive up, fists under rump
To patter-slap, to shape, to drive the bell
And start its voice athunder
In your bones and swarming through the air
To shake blue snows of summer sky
Invisible and drifting on the glare.
The bell swings traveling; you kick it on;
Returned, you thrust it, hungry-mouthed and lolling
Forth again, now lashing iron tongue
To lick its clangorous rims,
To bang, to detonate in glorious *pronunciamentos:*
I'm here! 'Tis me!
'Tis me who hooves the cannon bell!
To wake the summer dead out of their drowse.
'Tis me! A mouse
Of boy gone high in belfry dins!
Who with pure iron sound would douse your sins!
All, startled, listen, rouse,

And come, drift-dusted down the roads!
I summon you with freshly washed pink toes
And bell-creased crimsoned heel,
Upon my back I bicycle the wind
To rotor-thump the bombshell clangs!
Its great mouth hungers me;
I feed it feet.
Sprawled laughing, bell-sound in my lungs,
Prone underneath,
The sun all gone to shards, asplinter in my lids,
My mouth blood-rust from giving shout
To answer iron shout of bell:
Here's heaven! heaven! heaven!
Bang. Not hell. Not hell. Bang! Not hell!

Until the church below is full of summer breath
And priest then wanders forth to make discussion,
His nave much shaken to sense with wild concussion.
Now one must cease.
But sometimes in the uptilt, ever-frenzied dance, forgets;
So priest must send on mission yet another boy
To stop the bell
To still the belfry and the iron-spilled joy.
Now lie there yet awhile, fine lad, upon your back,
As bell tilts down to quiet, soft asimmer.
Long before loves and beds are known you have
    known this:
Bells are a loud communion,
Belfry-banging bells are bliss.

Glistered with holy sweat you lift your head
And send a bright salt golden rain down free from brow
With one shake, smiling.
It blesses the distant ground.
You touch the bell:
It trembles still with sound.
You touch the sky with glance:
It shivers bright with quakes you've given
It will, long gone days beyond, remember.
You laugh one last triumphant burst.
Great seas of prayer wait murmuring below
Carefully, holding to your soul
And sweet-bruised tender wits,
You descend the belfry stair,
Inexplicably wild with thirst.

What would I say of me,
If I were Epitaph?
That there were silly bones in him?
The grim but made him laugh?
The jolly made him serious?
The glum made him delirious?
That lawyers talked him sleepy,
And made him snooze at noon,
But bed was his by nine o'clock
So he could rise with moon?
And roll upon the meadows
While other people dreamed,
With windows up and chilly
He smiled and only steamed?
They sealed him in a coffin
But could not make him stay,
His laugh too large, his smile too wide
For any Death to lay?
No matter what the molder,
The maggot in his bin,
No measuring-worm could inch and cir-
Cumnavigate his grin?
If Universe should claim me
And keep me with a sleep
I'd open up my laughter
And drop the Abyss deep;
There we would lie all friendly,
The empty stars and I

And speak upon Creation
And with God occupy
The time that's left for burning,
A billion years to sup,
Then open wide God's laughter
And let Him eat me up.

The fence we walked between the years
Did balance us serene;
It was a place half in the sky where
In the green of leaf and promising of peach
We'd reach our hands to touch and almost touch
        that lie,
That blue that was not really blue.
If we could reach and touch, we said,
'Twould teach us, somehow, never to be dead.

We ached, we almost touched that stuff;
Our reach was never quite enough.
So, Thomas, we are doomed to die.
O, Tom, as I have often said,
How sad we're both so short in bed.
If only we had taller been,
And touched God's cuff, His hem,
We would not have to sleep away and go with them
Who've gone before,
A billion give or take a million boys or more
Who, short as we, stood tall as they could stand
And hoped by stretching thus to keep their land,
Their home, their hearth, their flesh and soul.
But they, like us, were standing in a hole.

O, Thomas, will a Race one day stand really tall
Across the Void, across the Universe and all?
And, measured out with rocket fire,
At last put Adam's finger forth

As on the Sistine Ceiling,
And God's great hand come down the other way
To measure Man and find him Good,
And Gift him with Forever's Day?
I work for that.
Short man. Large dream. I send my rockets forth
    between my ears,
Hoping an inch of Will is worth a pound of years.
Aching to hear a voice cry back along the universal Mall:
We've reached Alpha Centauri!
We're tall, O God, we're *tall!*

A NOTE ABOUT THE TYPE

This book was set in the film version of Optima, a typeface designed by Hermann Zapf from 1952 to 1955 and issued in 1958. In designing Optima, Zapf created a truly new type form—a cross between the classic roman and a sans-serif face. So delicate are the stresses and balances in Optima that it rivals sans-serif faces in clarity and freshness and old-style faces in variety and interest.

Composed by University Graphics, Inc., Shrewsbury, New Jersey; printed and bound by The Book Press, Inc., Brattleboro, Vermont. Typography and binding design by Clint Anglin.